London
Transport

in the 1960s

Michael H. C. Baker

Ian Allan
PUBLISHING

Contents

Front cover:
The Routemaster personified the 1960s, more than 2,000 being delivered, to several distinct styles. Their initial goal was to replace the trolleybuses. RM1200 passes under the disused wires in Surbiton on 9 May 1962, the first day without electric traction. *Geoff Rixon*

Back cover (upper):
The way forward appeared to be the OMO, multi-standee Merlin. The Red Arrow services, represented by MBA18 at Victoria alongside roofbox RT1879, were a success, but the entry of the Merlins into general service from 1968 proved to be anything but. *John Bishop*

Back cover, lower:
A train of 'A' stock, seen heading for Uxbridge on the Metropolitan Line. *Author*

Title page: RTWs working London's most famous route in just about its most famous setting in November 1965, shortly before Routemasters took over. *Author*

For John and Clive of Winterbourne High School, and for Barry and Sid of Whitgift Middle, who got me hooked and showed me the way

First published 2005

ISBN 0 7110 3072 3

© Michael H. C. Baker 2005

Published by Ian Allan Publishing

an imprint of Ian Allan Publishing Ltd, Hersham, Surrey KT12 4RG

Printed in England by Ian Allan Printing Ltd, Hersham, Surrey KT12 4RG

Code: 0509/B

Visit the Ian Allan Publishing website at www.ianallanpublishing.com

Foreword

MY first-hand observation of the London Transport scene in the 1960s was episodic. In 1960 I was still living at home, within the sound of RTs revving in Thornton Heath garage, although the decibels were somewhat less, or at any rate it was a rather less penetrating sound than that of the trams squealing around the sharp bend leading from the depot to the main London Road which had preceded it.

Public transport has always made a significant contribution to the noise of London and its suburbs. Petrol-engined buses, gone by the beginning of the 1950s, sounded very different from diesel-engined buses, RT (AEC) engines did not sound quite like RTL or RTW (Leyland) engines, and Routemasters, with several engine changes throughout their long careers, were different again. Peter Ackroyd, in his monumental *London, the Biography* (Vintage, 2001),

writes of the 'distinctive, ever changing noise which has characterised London for a thousand years'. By the middle of the 19th century Jane Carlyle, wife of Thomas, noted that a significant contributor to this noise was 'omnibuses, carriages, glass coaches, street coaches . . .'. By the end of the first decade of the 20th century the throb of the petrol engine and the grinding of gears was rapidly replacing the sound of horses' hooves — or, to quote Virginia Woolf, 'chimed into one sound, steel, blue, circular.' A notable element, the grinding of the steel wheels of the tramcar on steel rails, had disappeared in 1952, and it was perhaps ironic that the vastly quieter hum of electric motors and the swish of tyres of its successor, the trolleybus, should itself be replaced by the all-conquering, considerably noisier diesel bus 10 years later, just as the term 'noise pollution' was beginning to enter common usage.

Left: Saunders roofbox-bodied RT4220 stands on the forecourt of Thornton Heath garage in the early 1960s. Although Routemasters, such as RM337 inside the garage, began to appear in the Croydon area from the early 1960s, RTs (albeit not the roofbox variety) continued to work the extremely busy 109 into the 1970s. *Author*

Yet just as in Victorian times one could escape the noise of London even in its heart — 'turning into [the Inns of Court] . . . imparts to the relieved pedestrian the sensation of having put cotton in his ears and velvet soles on his boots,' as Charles Dickens reminds us in *Edwin Drood* — so one could still find silence in the 1960s. In the summer of 1961 I worked as a porter at Victoria station. Night duty officially ended at 6am, but there was little to do much after 1 o'clock, and one could usually stretch out on the seats of a train berthed overnight at one of the platforms and, hopefully, fall asleep. More than once I awoke around dawn, and before the first Circle Line train had clattered below stairs or the first bus left Gillingham Street garage I would stroll into St James's Park. Silence reigned. Then, as though at the behest of an unseen conductor (orchestral, not bus), the dawn chorus would burst forth from the treetops, echoing across the lake, the impossibly exotic flamingoes would preen their pink feathers preparing to bask in another day's adulation, and London would begin to awake.

I was at this time a student at Chelsea Art School and for the first time had a London postal address — in Battersea, I hasten to add, not Chelsea, for one could hardly live on that side of the river on a student grant. I travelled sometimes by Inner Circle, sometimes by number 19 bus, sometimes by the 11. Have you ever been to sea on a London bus? Not easy to do in the normal course of events, although Montgomery (as you'll discover in Chapter 13) did, and I've managed to get within a promenade's width of it in preserved STL2377 and RTL139 on trips from Cobham to the late, lamented Southsea

Spectacular. But with a bit of artistic licence, with which we art students were, of course, issued, it was possible to imagine one was some distance from dry land on the 19. Most mornings the RT on which I was travelling to college would come to a halt midway across Battersea Bridge, and from my upper-deck seat, if I looked east or west rather than straight down, I could see nothing but Thames water. Well if Whistler (the one with the Mother), who lived a few hundred yards away, could be imaginative, so could I.

In September 1963 I took up a teaching post in Hampstead — the Kilburn end rather than the posh end. This involved lengthy journeys on Green Line RFs. I soon learned to hold very tight if sitting on an outside seat as we rounded Hyde Park Corner and Marble Arch, and appreciated just why, in the early 1950s, buses and coaches had expanded in width from 7ft 6in to 8ft. By now, with the trolleybuses all gone, Routemasters were ousting RTLs and RTWs from many of the most heavily patronised Central London routes and were on their way to establishing their long-standing near-monopoly of Oxford Street. A visit to a friend in Ham presented the opportunity to ride a Routemaster coach on the 715. Then, as now, the stretch of the Thames from Richmond through Ham to Kingston was astonishingly rural. There were not many places in the London area where you could view from a red double-decker a herd of cows grazing, but such was the prospect across the water meadows at Ham if you took a ride on route 65 heading for Kingston. The 65, once home to elderly, worn-out ex-London General STLs, was an early conversion to RTs and would remain faithful to the type into the 1970s.

Bus-wise, Kingston was a rather extraordinary town at the beginning of the 1960s, for the great majority of the 'red bus' routes which served it were worked by single-deckers. Indeed, Kingston was the only garage in the whole Central Area which operated no double-deckers. There were three Country Area routes, the 406, 406A and the 418, which brought in RTs from Leatherhead and Reigate garages, and Fulwell

Left: A clerestory-roofed East London Line train about to leave New Cross station, 1963.
Ian Allan Library

4

supplied trolleybuses. For many years these had been postwar 'Q1s', but at the end prewar 'L3s' replaced them, the 'Q1s' emigrating to Spain. These, along with Isleworth 'K1s' and 'K2s', brought the London trolleybus system to a close in 1962, whereafter Routemasters went some way towards re-establishing the balance of double- versus single-deck motor buses.

In 1966 I became a bus driver. Not in London, although my vehicle was an AEC, albeit a Yeates-bodied Maudslay-badged coach. My journey began in Gillingham, Kent — Maidstone & District territory — and ended seven weeks later in Kabul, Afghanistan — bandit territory. I flew home as far as Moscow, a city with a sizeable tram fleet. On first acquaintance the little green single-deckers seemed to have practically nothing in common with London's big red double-deckers. However, a ride on one early in the morning — it was mid-summer, and a dawn thunderstorm had woken me — persuaded me otherwise, for the wooden slatted floor, the two-and-one seating, the hum of the motors and the clatter over the numerous crossings were all reminiscent of a standard London 'E1'. From Moscow I caught the overnight train to Leningrad and thence on over the border into Finland, where an elegant green, wood-burning Pacific replaced our big USSR diesel. Various ferries and trains (diesel, electric and steam) and one bus (an RT on the 109) would deposit me, five days later, in Thornton Heath.

The following summer, married, I moved to South Norwood and for the second time had a London postal address. Maeve, my wife, taught in a vast Comprehensive school in Catford, whilst I worked at several schools in Croydon and an

Above: An RT passing Southern Railway 4-LAV and BR-built 4-EPB electric multiple-units at South Croydon in the summer of 1969. *Author*

FE college in Stepney, where my students ranged from the son of an Afghan chief to the daughter of the engineer in charge of the locks and bridges in the docks. Getting to and from work for the pair of us encompassed just about everything from Southern Electric through RTs, Routemasters and Merlins (which were making considerable inroads into double-deck routes in the Elmers End, Beckenham and Catford areas) to the very last clerestory-roof carriages in ordinary service in the UK, on the East London line between New Cross Gate and Whitechapel.

My final move of the decade was to Oxted. Godstone CUV-C-registered RMLs worked the 410 from Bromley past Biggin Hill, down into Westerham and along the A25 through Limpsfield and Oxted to Redhill and Reigate, whilst Chelsham and East Grinstead provided RFs for the meandering routes around Oxted, Hurst Green and Limpsfield and out into the Surrey/Kent/Sussex Weald, where they met the dark green of Maidstone & District and the lighter green of Southdown.

As 1969 drew to a close so London's bus world was about to change forever. On 1 January 1970 all the green buses and the Green Line network passed from the control of 55 Broadway and were handed over to the National Bus Company under the title of London Country. Truly the end of an era.

Michael H. C. Baker
April 2005

Introduction

JUST as London as a city is unique, so are the big, red double-deck buses which have served it for 100 years. But by the end of the 1960s the London double-decker had achieved cult status. With world travel by jet airliner a practical proposition for anyone with a reasonable level of affluence tourism to London boomed as never before. It became Swinging London, the place to be. And one of the symbols of Swinging London, known by the end of the decade the world over, was the red double-decker. Perhaps, if you are of tender years, we ought to explain what was meant by 'Swinging London'.

For the first half of the century culture was divided into highbrow and lowbrow, or, to put it another way, it was class-based, and the average working- or lower-middle-class bus/tram/train traveller was assumed to be either poorly educated or not educated at all and therefore lacking in taste. In other words, uncultured. Then a pop group from Liverpool called The Beatles became phenomenally successful almost overnight; 'serious' music and art critics wrote about them, they took the USA and the rest of the world by storm, they turned out to be articulate, they appeared at the Royal Command Performance and, instead of being overawed by the occasion, they made fun of the rich people in the best seats, who loved being made fun of. The world was changed for ever.

What ordinary young people from Secondary Moderns and Comprehensives looked like and listened to became mainstream. Pop music and pop art, even if it didn't oust everything which had gone before, was in the ascendant. And there was nothing more popular — or at least more universally available — than public transport. Much of 1960s pop music was ephemeral and of the moment, but some of it resonates across age and background, speaks of its time, and has anchored itself forever in culture. One such song was 'Waterloo Sunset', by Ray Davies of The Kinks. Composed in 1967, its deceptively simple lyrics, with their references to Waterloo station and the Underground, was romantic, nostalgic — a perfect evocation of a particular part of London at a particular time. Bob Geldof, who knows a thing or two about culture and connecting with the public, puts it on a level with Wordsworth's poem 'Lines Composed on Westminster Bridge'.

The view from the bridges across the Thames has been celebrated by countless painters, especially since London became the hub of a great empire in Victorian times — Whistler, Monet and Van Gogh, to name just three non-Englishmen, for example. Any picture of a Thames bridge in Victorian times is bound to feature horse buses and trams, and any in the first half of the 20th century motor buses and electric trams. Some of the pop painters of the 1960s found the red double-decker irresistible, one of the best known being Allen Jones, who in 1962, in the brilliant, colourful style known as Royal College Pop, produced a series of canvases of bus interiors and exteriors. Another Royal College painter was Pauline Boty, beautiful and talented. She came from Carshalton, which meant as a schoolgirl she travelled each day on the 654 trolleybus. A stunning painter (and actress too), she just lost out to Julie Christie for the lead in *Darling* (no disgrace there) and died at the tragically early age of 27. Later Eduardo Ardizzoni, often regarded as the founder of Pop Art, would be commissioned by London Transport to design murals for Tottenham Court Road tube station. Allen Jones began his studies at Hornsey, and later taught at Croydon Art School; Ray Davies was also a student there, while 'Edward' Ardizzoni was brought up in the East End. All knew their London and its suburbs and the buses, trams, trolleybuses and Underground which served them intimately. Neasden, which until the 1960s had been famous chiefly for its Underground and Tube depot, now became celebrated as the home of Twiggy, the world's most popular fashion model and 'the Face of the 'Sixties'. She would regularly pose in front of or on board a Routemaster, but you were most unlikely to find her actually travelling on one.

Whilst on the subject of the Routemaster, it is, perhaps, something of a myth that its predecessor, the

RT family — you'll see the connection — was particularly long-lived. It was and it wasn't. Certainly great play was made of the fact that, by the time the last RTs finished passenger service in 1979, the type had been in service for 40 years. But none of the final handful dated back to before 1948, and many, especially the RTL and RTW Leylands, did not even match the 18- to 20-year lifespan achieved by their longest-serving forebears, the STs, LTs and STLs.

It is interesting to examine why so many of the RT family were sold prematurely by London Transport. In the first place the number of new buses needed was over-estimated. By the mid-1950s it was clear that the twin forces of private motoring and staying at home (if this can be described as a force) to watch television were inexorably forcing down patronage. The long strike of 1958 made things worse, although it probably only hastened the process.

After the last trolleybuses had been replaced by RMs of lower capacity (except for a handful of 72-seat lengthened RMLs allocated to Finchley in 1961) RMs and then RMLs began to replace the RT family. The RTLs and the RTWs which they ousted from many of the most heavily patronised Central London routes — 11, 15, 22 etc — were in excellent condition. Were these later Routemasters necessary? The Leylands may not have been as popular with drivers as were the AEC RTs, but they could have served London quite happily until the end of the decade, by which time they would have been between 16 and 22 years old (although the last batch of RTLs did not enter service until 1958).

A number of both standard and lengthened Routemasters were fitted out as Green Line coaches. Despite these being the most comfortable double-deckers yet seen on the streets of London, Green Line figures were hæmorrhaging rapidly, and all ended their days prematurely, being demoted to bus and trainer duties. Other RMLs were put into Country Area service, and although none of these

fulfilled their expected lifespan in this role, a great many were bought back by London Transport and worked on into the third millennium — which demonstrated just how long the classic Chiswick-designed double-decker could serve the capital, given the opportunity. Few plans ever go quite as anticipated, and one can be sure that any prediction will likely be substantially wrong. Perhaps one should not be too hard on the soothsayers' section of LTE — a vital but rather secretive department located in the former officers' mess of a World War 2 aerodrome in Hertfordshire. Yet the huge variation in the time served in passenger service of identical members of the RT class, ranging from four to 31 years, does seem extraordinary.

*   *   *

If at the beginning of the 1950s Britain was still recovering from World War 2 and had not yet abolished rationing, a decade later a generation that had not known the war was approaching school-leaving age. The spectre of two years' National Service was about to be abolished, their parents did not lack for employment, they had pocket money and they might well have a Saturday job in a shop or coffee bar. They were affluent. In the words of Prime Minister Harold Macmillan in 1960, they had 'never had it so good'. And one of the first things you did when you had money was to buy your own transport. To start with this would be a motorbike or motor scooter — a Vespa or Lambretta, probably; like the big red bus, both became icons of the age.

Above: Green Line relief RTs on layover in the forecourt of Gillingham Street garage, Victoria. By the end of the 1960s patronage on the Green Line network was in serious decline and there would be less and less need for extra double-deck vehicles at peak hour or any other time. *Author*

Then you'd move up to your own four wheels. So we had the ironic situation that, whilst the London bus was regarded with great affection, fewer and fewer people actually travelled on it. Car ownership and travel went on increasing, despite the widespread introduction of parking meters — remember the Beatles song, 'Lovely Rita, Meter Maid'? The first parking meters appeared, in Mayfair, in 1958.

The year 1962 saw the end of what had once been the most extensive trolleybus system in the world, despite increasing but still fairly minimal concerns about pollution from the petrol and diesel engine. In order to reduce costs, at the expense of longer boarding times and thus yet greater congestion, the conductor began to disappear. One-man operation had begun in the Country Area in the mid-1950s and first appeared in the Central Area, in the outer suburbs from Kingston, Norbiton, Fulwell, and North Street (Romford) garages, in November 1964.

By the mid-1960s London Transport was struggling to overcome the problems caused by traffic congestion and staff shortage. The latter arose from the fact that wages (and living costs) were higher in the capital than in the rest of the country — a situation with which London Transport had not really come to terms. The difficulty of attracting and

Above: On 8 May 1962 London's last trolleybuses gave way to Routemasters in Stage 14 of the replacement programme. Two of Isleworth depot's all-Leyland 'K1s', Nos 1113 and 1065, are seen on the turning circle at Hounslow on 5 May 1962, three days before both their end and that of Isleworth depot itself. *Leslie Sandler*

retaining labour in booming economic conditions meant that London Transport was hæmorrhaging workers to more lucrative jobs with less anti-social hours; at the beginning of 1966 it was 12% understaffed. In much the same position were such long-established chassis/body manufacturers as AEC (at Southall), Park Royal and Weymann (at Addlestone), which firms had been responsible for supplying the bulk of the postwar double-deck fleet.

Much of the congestion was down to a huge increase over the preceding 10 years in the number of private cars on the road. At the busiest times there were 26,500 more in 1966 than there had been in 1956; by contrast there were 1,700 fewer buses. Yet the cars, occupying 80% of the road space, carried only one third of the travellers. Fare increases (implemented in 1966) and reduced schedules angered staff as well as passengers, such that overtime and rest-day working temporarily ceased; until the dispute was settled some services were withdrawn, and (foreshadowing events two decades later) private operators allowed to fill the gaps. Although the immediate consequences were not as grave as those of the 1958 strike, significant changes were afoot, among them the accelerated replacement of conductors, the loss of the Country Area to the newly formed National Bus

Company and a change in the ownership of London Transport itself.

On 18 April 1966 one-man operation (OMO) reached the heart of London with the inauguration of Red Arrow service 500, running between Victoria and Hyde Park Corner. It was operated by high-capacity AEC Swift single-deckers (which London Transport insisted were 'Merlins') with bodywork — by Strachans (a new name in London) — seating 25 and with standing room for a further 48.

The move to single-deck OMO was not merely an experiment. In September 1966 London Transport produced its Bus Reshaping Plan, which was intended to transform public transport in London and its suburbs. Designed to address both the increasing staff shortages and traffic congestion, as well as taking into account the 'short-hop' nature of most passenger journeys, the Reshaping Plan proposed the shortening of major trunk routes and the replacement of their outer ends with flat-fare OMO services feeding into modal interchange points based on Underground stations. London Transport envisaged that those double-deck routes which remained would eventually be converted to OMO, which meant the eventual withdrawal not only of the entire RT family but also of the Routemaster. It did not look as if the RM would be anything like as long-lived as the RT.

The Wilson Government had announced a 25% grant towards each one-man bus registered after 1 August 1968, and with one-man operation of double-deckers yet to be agreed by the unions, many

of the replacements for the RTs and Routemasters would be single-deckers, even on the busiest Central London routes. However, the next generation of double-decker was already being evaluated, and as early as 1965 route 24, running from Pimlico to Hampstead Heath, saw the introduction of what to London eyes were very strange-looking buses — Park Royal-bodied Leyland Atlanteans. There was, of course, nothing strange in London about Leyland buses with Park Royal bodies, but these had standard provincial bodies, plain to look at and internally poorly appointed, with the engine in a bustle at the back. Similarly bodied green buses, on Daimler Fleetline chassis, took up work at East Grinstead garage. Both types still employed conductors, but, with power-operated doors at the front beside the driver, they were intended for eventual OMO use. Much more promising was the entry into service in 1967 of FRM1, a rear-engined version of the Routemaster. But times were changing at a bewildering pace; the days when London could design, build or commission its own bus chassis and bodies were coming to an end, and FRM1 would remain unique. The following year saw the entry into general service of the Merlin, which in so doing would kill the concept of a London bus quite different from anyone else's. Basically similar to the first batch, used on Red Arrow route 500, the production buses combined the same standard 36ft-long, rear-engined single-deck AEC Swift chassis (albeit modified for London use) with bodywork designed by London Transport and produced by Metro-Cammell. There were a number of variations, some for Country Area service. A shorter version (which London Transport acknowledged as a Swift) appeared at the end of 1969 and was bodied by several builders. Both types were monumentally disastrous.

Throughout the 1960s the RT family was reduced in size. The Leylands were the first to disappear entirely, the last RTW ending passenger service in 1966, the last RTL two years later. However, on 31 December 1969 there remained at work many hundreds of RTs, both in the Country Area and the Central Area, the oldest now into their third decade. The crisis caused by the unsuitability and unreliability of the Merlins and the Swifts would ensure that the RT would linger on in passenger service in the suburbs until the 1970s were almost over.

In April 1965 the Greater London Council came into being and with it plans to reduce the cost of bus and Underground travel — a brave attempt which

Drive a London Bus

A secure job for men
aged 21 years and over with experience
of driving heavy vehicles, and 23 years and over
with other driving experience

	BASIC WAGE	Average weekly wage for rostered duties (42 hours)
ON APPOINTMENT	£10-18-0	£12-16-2
AFTER I YEAR	£11-10-0	£13-9-10

- FREE TRAVEL ON AND OFF DUTY
- SICK PAY
- PENSION SCHEME FOR MEN
- FREE UNIFORM

Apply to the LONDON TRANSPORT RECRUITMENT CENTRE, Griffith House, 280 Marylebone Road, N.W.1

Above: An RT emerges from the partially completed Hammersmith Flyover, one of the measures designed to deal with London's ever-growing traffic problems. Competing for road space are an Austin A40, a VW 'Beetle' and an Austin A35. *Ian Allan Library*

Below: One of the prototype Red Arrow one-man-operated Merlins in Park Lane. *Author's collection*

Above: An experimental rear-engined Atlantean (XA class) and an RT with roof-mounted number box, seen at Trafalgar Square. *Author*

Below: The solitary rear-engined Routemaster, FRM1, at Victoria, 22 July 1967. *Gerald Mead*

Above: A big red London double-decker about to set off for a new life across the Atlantic. Bought by the British Travel & Holidays Association in 1964, RTL1176 was seen as the ideal vehicle to tour the United States as a 'Come to Britain' information centre. *Ian Allan Library*

would be frustrated by Central Government but which would resurface some 30-odd years later and prove its worth. There had been a time in the 1950s when the notion of abolishing the Country Area and absorbing its fleet into the Central Area red one had been seriously contemplated. Instead the wheel was to turn in the opposite direction, and at the end of 1967 it was announced that the Country Area and the Green Line network would be taken out of London Transport control and handed over to the National Bus Company. This duly took place on 1 January 1970 with the formation of London Country Bus Services Ltd.

In 1962 the last of the Metropolitan Line 'T'-stock trains — compartment-type, brown-painted and quite different from everything else on the Underground system — ceased work, as did the Bo-Bo electric locomotives. In 1968 the first completely new Tube line for many years, the Victoria Line, opened from Walthamstow to Highbury & Islington. It was soon extended to Warren Street and then, a year later, to Victoria. Finally, in 1971, it tunnelled under the Thames and, penetrating southwards into territory which had always been poorly served by sub-surface trains, reached Brixton. Automatic fare collection was installed and the trains were automatically controlled, although there was still a driver in the front cab. The Tube network would continue to expand — albeit more slowly than had been hoped — in the following decades.

Left: Roofbox RT3187, RT3929 and a Routemaster at Waterloo c1969. *Author*

Below: Metropolitan Line 'T' stock near Neasden, bound for Stanmore. *Ian Allan Library*

Right: A Routemaster and a cable car during 'London Week' in San Francisco, November 1962. RML898 had arrived in California by way of the Panama Canal. *Ian Allan Library*

• 1 •

The Trolleybus in Decline

THE year 1960 was one of highs and lows for advocates of electric propulsion — doom and gloom on the streets of London but plenty to cheer about on the railways. The silent, smooth riding, pollution-free, expensive-to-run, inflexible trolleybus continued its retreat, while electric trains replaced steam on the Metropolitan line to Chesham and also began to work to Amersham, and fourth-rail electrification was extended deep into Metroland, as far as Watford South Junction. In this chapter and the next we'll look at the last days of the London trolleybus, and in Chapter 3 electric trains.

The decade opened with trolleybuses already gone from much of East London and the suburbs beyond, albeit still with a considerable presence, whilst the North and West London networks remained intact. South of the river, where trams had lasted into the 1950s and where there had never been a plethora of trolleybus routes, the Dartford area and the Crystal Palace–Sutton services had been the first to go, in March 1959.

So why did the trolleybus have to die? At least one of the reasons — inflexibility — seems, at the beginning of the 21st century, to matter far less than it did 50 years ago. The fact is that certain traffic corridors will, short of an earthquake or nuclear holocaust, always carry a vast number of people. One can think of many such ancient main roads coming in through the country and cutting through the suburbs and into the centre of London, to which this applies — from Coulsdon through Purley and Croydon, Streatham and Brixton, the Uxbridge Road through Southall, Ealing, Acton and Shepherds Bush, the Edgware Road through Colindale, Cricklewood, Maida Vale and Marble Arch, from Waltham Cross through Edmonton, Tottenham, Stoke Newington and Dalston, and from Barking through East Ham, Canning Town, Poplar and the Commercial Road, to name but five. All of these were once served by an intensive tram service, some later by trolleybuses, and some are once again being considered as possible tram routes.

Another reason for getting rid of the trolleybus system was that all the ancillary equipment — the overhead and its supporting poles, feeders, substations, etc — which it had inherited from the trams was reaching the end of its life and would cost a huge sum to replace. Part of the inflexibility of the trolleybus was its need to slow down whenever it came to a junction where routes converged or diverged; if it went too fast then it could dewire. However, it might well be argued that, given that all traffic has to slow at junctions, this was of little consequence.

Originally most tram systems, like that of the London County Council (LCC), had been operated by local authorities, which provided the electricity, so if the trams made a profit everyone benefited. However, by the 1960s electricity, now provided by way of the national grid, had to be bought, and this made operation of trolleybuses, particularly on the less heavily patronised routes, more expensive than that of motor buses. There were, of course, arguments against a dependence on a fuel which both came from overseas (where the price might escalate) and would one day run out. But these were long-term considerations — no-one knew exactly *how* long — and carried little weight.

Trolleybus advocates raised the issue of pollution and the fact that the London trolleybus, even though the vast majority of the fleet dated back to prewar or early wartime years, was still seen as a comfortable, up-to-date vehicle, unlike the trams had been in their last years.

Perhaps the most important factor, superficial though it might seem, was that the trolleybus was out of fashion. Systems which had once been the pride of the towns and cities where they operated — one thinks particularly of Bournemouth, Belfast and Bradford — would succumb, and so would London, despite being the world's largest. It was certainly true that as systems all over Britain shut down so manufacturers of trolleybuses and their ancillary equipment either went out of business or switched to something else. But abroad it was different.

Above: One of the postwar 'Q1' trolleybuses, No 1781, speeds over the Thames away from Kingston on its way to Twickenham, shortly before making the much longer journey to Santander in Spain, where it would work until 1974. *Author*

Left: Having completed its London career, 'Q1' trolleybus 1830 is swung aboard ship, bound for a new life in sunny Spain. *Ian Allan Library*

In countries as diverse as Greece, Switzerland, the USA and the USSR the trolleybus flourished. And just as we were entering an era where mainland European manufacturers were beginning to challenge British motor-bus manufacturers, so, surely, it would have been possible to keep UK trolleybuses running by turning to foreign suppliers. But it was not to be, and if you want to ride on a trolleybus in the UK today you have to visit museums such as Carlton Colville, Sandtoft or the Black Country, where dedicated enthusiasts have lovingly cared for and restored the survivors of the once-great systems.

The first closure of 1960 took place on the night of 2/3 February and saw the end of routes 557, 669, 685, 689 and 690. Route 557 (there were far fewer 5xx routes than those in the 6xx series) ran between Chingford Mount and Liverpool Street. Worked by Walthamstow depot, it was one of the busiest in the East End, with a frequency of between three and five minutes. It was worked by various classes, ranging from DGY-registered 'D2s' to FXH-registered 'N1s'. Some 34 trolleys were withdrawn from Walthamstow, and 80 from West Ham. With the withdrawal of the 669 and the 685 North Woolwich lost its trolleybuses just as those on the opposite shore, connected by the Woolwich Free Ferry, had gone 11 months earlier. The northern terminus of the 685 was Walthamstow, that of the 669 Stratford. The 689 and 690 were short circular routes, operating in opposite directions from Stratford and known as the East Ham circulars. Stratford Broadway, once one of the busiest places on the trolleybus network, was now left with just two routes, the 697 and 699, and these would go in two months' time.

The 26/27 April conversions involved these last two Stratford routes, which linked Chingford Mount with the Victoria & Albert Docks. The 699, the highest-numbered London trolleybus route, had its origins in tram route 99, inaugurated by West Ham Corporation in 1912 to relieve pressure on service 97, worked jointly by West Ham and Walthamstow corporations. The level of attention paid by enthusiasts, local citizens and officialdom varied with each closure, but a nice gesture on 26 April was the use of highly decorated 'E2' No 622 as the very last trolleybus to enter West Ham depot, just as it had been the first, back in June 1937. Three other conversions took place at this time — the 687 from the Victoria & Albert Docks to Walthamstow, the 623 from Woodford to Manor House and the 625 from Woodford to Winchmore Hill. With each closure the oldest trolleybuses were withdrawn and the newer ones moved on to serve a little while longer, in turn replacing older vehicles which were driven to Colindale, where a scrapyard had been set up behind the depot. The Dartford vehicles ended their days at Charlton, where the trams and a number of motor buses had also been broken up.

Trolleybuses had now gone from North East London, and conversions now switched westwards. Also lost was the 611, which connected picturesque Highgate Village with the slightly less picturesque Moorgate. The final part of the journey north from the City involved climbing the 1-in-10 Highgate Hill, whence one had, as Dick Whittington knew only too well, a magnificent view over London. Just as the trolleybuses operating the steep 654 Crystal Palace route were fitted with special braking equipment, so were those which worked the 611, in this case Classes

J3 and L1, based at Highgate depot. Various reasons were suggested for the abandonment of the Highgate Village route before any of the others worked from Highgate depot, but, whatever, the final journey was worked by decorated 'L1' No 1360 on 19 July. The brakes fitted to standard Routemasters were deemed perfectly adequate for the motor buses which were sent to Highgate to inaugurate the replacement route 271, which, uniquely in later years, exactly replicated the 611 in its entirety.

Much nearer home, the last trolleybuses disappeared from the streets of Croydon, and from Mitcham, Tooting, Wandsworth and Putney on 19 July. It had been intended that they would last rather longer, but the construction of the Hammersmith flyover was one factor which brought about an earlier demise. The 630 — the London route I knew best, having frequently carried me to school — had for most of its life borne London's most famous destination, 'NEAR WILLESDEN JUNCTION', although in the last few years this had been replaced by the rather more mundane (and no more accurate) 'HARLESDEN'. The 'D2s' which for over 20 years had worked out of Hammersmith depot had been supplanted by 'F1' Leylands from Hanwell which had refused to go any further west and 'K1s' and 'K2s' from the mysterious east, so that at the end the only originals were a handful of 'P1' Leylands, examples of the very last prewar-designed London trolleybus. There were only 25 of them, and they popped up at a number of depots. Hammersmith had the very last of all — No 1721, delivered in October 1941. A little surprisingly, none of the 'P1s' made it with the 'K1' and 'K2' Leylands to see out the London trolleybus from Isleworth depot. The 630, at 14.65 miles, is generally regarded as London's longest trolleybus route, for although the 655 from Acton Vale to Clapham Junction was a little longer this did not operate its full length except during rush hours.

The 626 peak-hour service from Acton to Clapham Junction and the 628 from Craven Park (just up the road from Harlesden) to Clapham Junction also disappeared on 19 July. These were routes much favoured by trainspotters, linking as they did Clapham Junction, the busiest station in the British Isles, with the exotically named North Pole Junction, a short distance from the big girder bridge which carried Scrubs Lane over the Grand Union Canal and the main line out of Paddington, with excellent views of Old Oak Common engine shed and carriage depot, whilst just up the road was the 630 terminus and the maze of lines at Willesden Junction. Astonishing to think back to the days when I would alight from a 630 and walk down the slope to spend unchallenged hours standing at the trackside as 'Kings', 'Castles', 'Britannias', '61xxs', pannier tanks etc steamed by. Nowadays this area is the location of

Above: 'L3' No 1553 of Highgate depot c1960
at Chancery Lane, just about the furthest into the
heart of London the trolleybus network penetrated.
John Glover collection

Eurostar depot, and I doubt if even a personally signed permit from God would get me inside.

Unlike the earliest trolleybus-replacement schemes all those of 1960 featured Routemasters, and by mid-summer 1960 well over 400 were in service.

Late autumn saw the London trolleybus disappear from its most westerly terminus, Uxbridge. This was served by the 607, which linked it with Shepherd's Bush. The route was remarkable in several respects, most of all because it was the busiest of the entire network. By now there could be no doubting that the trolleybus was doomed, for this was a route ideally suited to high-capacity electrically powered vehicles. For a time during the morning and evening peaks you could stand anywhere along its length and expect to see a trolleybus come by every minute. Until it ceased, on the evening of 8 November, it had an allocation of 66 vehicles Mondays to Fridays, with two more on Saturdays. Operated by Hanwell depot, it passed the AEC works at Southall, opposite the famous Iron Bridge (with prominent advertisement for AEC products) which carried the main line from Paddington to Reading, the West of England and South Wales. The Uxbridge Road was one of those trunk routes which have always provided a huge passenger potential. Before the trolleybuses the 'Felthams' of London United Tramways had worked the road (service 7), with considerable distinction, but nothing could sway London Transport from its anti-

tram philosophy, and in 1936 the 'Felthams' were sent south of the river to Telford Avenue. Class D2 trolleybuses were provided initially but were quickly replaced by the more powerful 'F1s'. Ironically these were Leylands, and AEC trolleybuses never normally ran past the AEC works, although it could be argued that the postwar 'Q1' class, a number of which (both HYM and LYH series) were allocated to Hanwell, were really AECs, although they were officially BUTs. A most unusual trolleybus which was a regular on the 607 was No 1671, the unique twin-steering 'X7', distinguishable also by its Lancashire (rather than London) registration. Such is the continuing potential of the Uxbridge Road that there are serious proposals that the wheel should turn full circle and trams once again run along it.

Also withdrawn on 8 November was route 655. Worked by Hanwell depot (but never by the 8ft-wide 'Q1s', on account of the narrowness of one section of the route at Boston Road, between Hanwell and Brentford), this ran from Hanwell to Hammersmith except during weekday peak hours, when it was extended to Acton Vale in the west and Clapham Junction in the east.

• 2 •

The End of the Trolleybus

NOW we're into 1961, and the London trolleybus is speeding towards its final destination. Seven more routes — 513/613, 517/617, 615, 639 and 653 — disappeared on the night of 31 January. The twin 513/613 operated from Hampstead Heath to Parliament Hill Fields via Holborn, the former taking the Holborn Loop by way of Grays Inn Road, the latter via Farringdon Road. The other twins, the 517/617, ran from North Finchley to Holborn, the former via Grays Inn Road, the latter via Farringdon Road. The 615 ran from Parliament Hill Fields to Moorgate, the 639 from Hampstead Heath to Moorgate. Finally the 653, one of London's most interesting trolleybus routes, connected Tottenham Court Road with Aldgate. The two termini were not that far apart, but the 653 linked them by a great sweeping arc which took in Camden Town, Holloway, Finsbury Park, Manor House, Stamford Hill, Clapton, Hackney, Cambridge Heath, Bethnal Green and Whitechapel in its 64-minute journey. Intensively used over its eastern section, it ran every two/three minutes between Finsbury Park and Aldgate. It was the East End's last trolleybus route. When I paid my first visit in the mid-1950s the docks were still the busiest in the world, with a dense network of trolleybus routes along the East India Dock Road, the Whitechapel Road, Limehouse, a world I had known only through wartime newsreels of Blitz devastation, Edgar Lustgarten crime films, documentaries on the river police — Dickensian slums, cosmopolitan, multi-racial and as far removed from my bit of the London suburbs as could be imagined.

Spring brought the end for four more routes, serving North London, three reaching Waltham Cross, the most northerly extent of the trolleybus network. These were the 627, 659 and 679, which terminated respectively at Tottenham Court Road, Holborn and Smithfield. Edmonton, Wood Green and Highgate were the depots involved. The fourth was the 629, Enfield's solitary trolleybus route and another which terminated in Tottenham Court Road

(or, to be more accurate, just off it, in Fitzroy Street). Closure came on 25 April. By this time no trolleybuses numbered below 1000 were still at work, and all those working out of Wood Green and Edmonton were Leyland 'K1s', 'K2s' and 'K3s'. These latter were in one sense throwbacks, for although they were very nearly the last prewar type to be delivered — only the P1s, which had identical chassis but Metro-Cammell bodies, were newer — they had earlier-style bodies with squared-off corners to practically all the windows, those at the front making them look particularly old-fashioned compared with Highgate's 'L'-class vehicles and Edmonton's own small batch of 'P1s'. The end of the 627 meant the end of Highgate as a trolleybus depot; it had once been home to more trolleys than any other London depot, and throughout the 1940s and until 1951 had also been a tram depot. The small (25-strong) 'M1' class, variously described as of unitary construction or with light-weight AEC chassis, finished service when Highgate closed, having migrated there from East London.

By this time London's newest trolleybuses, the 'Q1s', had found buyers in Spain, so instead of lasting into the late 1960s the Isleworth and Fulwell routes which they worked would for their last few months be operated by prewar vehicles, 'K1s' and 'K2s' (but, oddly, no 'K3s') going to Isleworth and 'L3s' to Fulwell.

Whilst on the subject of the 'Ks' it is impossible not to comment on the different attitudes adopted to minor variations by the motor-bus and the trolleybus departments of London Transport. Throughout virtually the entire period of prewar trolleybus production the standard motor bus was the STL. That was it. Every AEC double-decker bus, from the first, delivered in January 1933, to the last, in September 1939, was an STL. In broadly the same period, from October 1935 until December 1939, there were no fewer than 12 varieties of AEC trolleybus. The motor-bus equivalent of the STL was the STD class of Leyland Titans, just 100 of them; there were 11 varieties of Leyland trolleybus. And the

Left: Training of new trolleybus drivers continued until a few weeks before the final withdrawal. 'K1' No 1118 of Isleworth slips past another trainer, RT2998, as it turns into Chiswick Works, 4 April 1961. *Author*

point is that, while there were all sorts of body, chassis and engine variations within the STL class, each was still called an STL, whereas in the trolley-bus fleet, whenever there was a minor variation, out was trotted a new class designation. The 'K1s' and 'K2s' had absolutely identical bodies and chassis, the only difference being that the 'K1s' had Metro-Vick controllers, the 'K2s' English Electric. The only variation between the 'K2s' and the 'K3s' that I can detect was in the position of the sidelights. A similar situation applied with the chassisless MCW 'Ls'. There were variations, the chief concerning the windows, which on the 'L3s' were rubber-mounted and curved at the bottom. But you can bet that if these had been motor buses they would all have been lumped into the same designation. But the trolleybus department, manned by ex-tram men, went very much its own way, not least when it came to livery — but we won't get into that one!

Stage 11, on Tuesday 19 July, saw the last trolley-bus route, the 649, withdrawn from the network's most northerly extremity, Waltham Cross; its City terminus was Liverpool Street. I expect you knew that Waltham Cross got its name from the resting place of the body of Henry II's queen, Eleanor, as the grieving king brought her back to London, the last (before interment in Westminster Abbey) being Charing Cross. The Sunday before the end (of the 649, not Queen Eleanor) saw the end of the only trolleybus route with an A suffix, the 649A, which ran each Sunday between Liverpool Street and Wood Green. Two other Wood Green routes, the 543 and 643, which both terminated at Holborn (one going anti-clockwise, the other clockwise), were replaced by the 243. Finally the 647, which ran

between Stamford Hill and the London Docks, was replaced by the 67. Wood Green and Stamford Hill depots now operated Routemasters, and Liverpool Street and the Docks saw trolleybuses no more. Now it was the turn of many of the numerous 'K1s' and 'K2s' to go for scrap at Colindale, although others moved westwards to Isleworth.

Which brings us to Stage 12, the last of 1961, leaving only two to go. On the night of 7 November four routes — 521 (the last 5xx-series route), 621, 609 and 641 — succumbed to the Routemaster. The first two, sharing a northern terminus at North Finchley, were yet another pair following exactly the same route save for circumnavigating the Holborn Loop in opposite directions. The 609 ran between Moorgate and Barnet, and the 641 between Moorgate and Winchmore Hill. The 641 had throughout its career worked closely with the 629, which ran between Winchmore Hill and Tottenham Court Road, their ways parting at Manor House, but because of the introduction of a one-way traffic system at Tottenham Court Road the 629 had gone six months earlier. The 641 had been operated by Wood Green, meaning that yet more 'K1s' and 'K2s' met their end, leaving only the Isleworth contingent to last into 1962.

The 609, 521 and 621 had been worked by Finchley depot, although Highgate also worked the 609 on Sundays; since Stage 10 it had provided Routemasters. Otherwise in their last days the handsome 'L3s' had a virtual monopoly of the three routes. No 1464 became the last trolleybus in the City of London when it worked the final 521 away from Holborn. Two significant developments accompanied the conversion to motor buses. For the first time the lengthened 72-seat Routemaster went into service,

15 being provided by Finchley for the 104, the replacement for the 609. Their originally intended classification of ER (extended Routemaster) was changed to RML before they took up work. The 'via' points on their blinds appeared in lower case. Comparative tests had been carried out with the then-current all-upper-case version; although these were inconclusive, fashion determined that lower-case won the day, and a number of routes (not just trolleybus replacements) were so equipped from 8 November. Eventually lower-case became universal, but it was a lengthy process, pursued as blinds wore out or routes changed.

As 1962 opened there were only two more conversions to go. The BRCW-bodied AEC 'N1s' and Park Royal-bodied 'N2s' had taken up residence at Colindale and Stonebridge depots, having migrated thither from East London, but their time was now up. These were handsome vehicles, very like the 'L3s' but with detail differences; I had several journeys on

them in their last few weeks in service and found it hard to believe that such smooth running, well-appointed, far-from-shabby vehicles were about to be scrapped. Tuesday 2 January saw the end of routes 645 from Canons Park — the nearest trolleybuses got to Aldenham Works — to Barnet, the 662 Sudbury to Paddington, the 660 from North Finchley to Hammersmith and the 666 from Edgware to Hammersmith.

Heavy snow had fallen during the last day of 1961 and was still thick on the ground, a good deal of it having turned to slush, on 2 January. I can't be sure, but I'm pretty certain there were further showers, for even though the sun came out briefly on the final afternoon a number of vehicles were still liberally covered in snow, in some cases their indicators barely visible. The wide forecourt of Stonebridge depot was still frozen and the snow crunched under the wheels as the trolleybuses — and the RTs on route 112 — gingerly manœuvred. Finchley, Stonebridge and

Above: Lower case for 'via' points was introduced with Stage 12 of the trolleybus-replacement programme, on 8 November 1961. Newly overhauled RT247, one of the very early postwar RTs, by now fitted with a later body, lays over in the forecourt of Finchley depot/garage on revised route 125 on the first morning of operation. Poking their noses outside are several RMLs, this being the lengthened Routemasters' first day in passenger service. *Author*

Left: In their final years 'N1s' which had served most of their careers in East London moved westwards, a group being seen at Colindale depot in 1961. *Author*

Above: Edmonton 'K1/2'- and 'K3'-class Leylands awaiting breaking-up behind Colindale depot in 1962. *Author*

Right: Stage 13 was effected on 2/3 January 1962, during some of the severest weather London had experienced for a number of years. 'N1' and 'N2' trolleybuses stand at the back of Stonebridge depot during the afternoon of 2 January, waiting to take up their final duties during the evening rush hour. They would have one more journey, the short one westwards, to be broken up at Colindale. *Author*

Colindale were now all gone, although, of course, large numbers of trolleys could still be found in various states of decay and demolition behind Colindale depot.

The London trolleybus had just five months to go. At the end there were the 657, the only route worked by Isleworth depot, which ran from Shepherd's Bush to Hounslow, the 667 from Hammersmith to Hampton Court, and the five Kingston routes, 601-5, all the responsibility of Fulwell. Isleworth provided Leyland 'K1s' and 'K2s', Fulwell AEC 'L3s', although several 'L1s' and 'L2s' had also survived long enough to be transferred to Fulwell and did appear, on occasions in passenger service.

The very last day, as has become customary since, with the end of various RT routes and even more so with the final withdrawals of the Routemaster in the 21st century, saw all sorts of celebrations and commemorations. Most notable was the re-emergence of the original 'Diddler', trolleybus No 1, which had been preserved as part of London Transport's collection of historic vehicles. It had been at Fulwell depot since March, being checked over, and was deemed (not without some doubts) as just about fit to make one ceremonial tour of Kingston, after which it was immediately towed back by one of the service fleet's green AEC lorries to Clapham Museum. It was not just enthusiasts who turned out in numbers but also the general public, and the press made much of the occasion. The *Wimbledon Borough News* noted: 'London's last trolleybus was given a magnificent send-off by hundreds of people outside

Wimbledon Town Hall on Tuesday night. Dozens of people had waited for hours for the honour of a seat on the last bus, and many were disappointed. Almost all the sightseers had cameras and flashguns.' On the last 657 from Isleworth depot there was hardly room for passengers, so voluminous were the paper chains, balloons, and flags filling both upper and lower decks.

The very last trolleybus from Fulwell depot, 'L3' No 1521, was driven by 70-year-old Albert West, the oldest driver at the depot. Clearly one was encouraged to carry on with such a responsible job well beyond the age of 65 if one was capable — no ageism there. His conductor, who in the official London Transport picture looks much the same age, was Ronald Gadsby. Inevitably No 1521 lost a number of fittings to souvenir-hunters and was far from complete when handed over to scrap merchant George Cohen. However, fate looked kindly on No 1521, as it surely should have, for Cohen's did not break it. When I last saw No 1521 it was in splendid

form, fully restored and repainted into wartime condition as it was when new and serving in the East End, for Cohen's donated it to the London Trolleybus Preservation Society, and it now lives in that mecca for the trolleybus enthusiast, Carlton Colville Transport Museum, on the outskirts of Lowestoft in faraway East Anglia.

What else was left? There was precious little demand in the UK for second-hand trolleybuses; although ex-Brighton four-wheelers found further employment in Maidstone and Bournemouth, for example, no-one wanted high-capacity six-wheelers. The 'Q1s', of course, had gone to Spain, where the last was not taken out of service until 1978. Some of the trams withdrawn in the 1930s and early '40s had become holiday homes and the like, but building regulations and greater prosperity denied this option to the trolleybus. The remaining overhead was soon taken down, and the tower wagons, built as maintenance vehicles but whose final duty was dismantling, were sold off or followed the trolleys to the scrap heap. The poles were often adapted as lamp standards and lasted a good deal longer; indeed, a few can still be found in various parts of London. Most depots were converted to bus garages. There are various other relics. Recently I revisited after an interval of perhaps 20 years the girder bridge carrying Scrubs Lane over the main line out of Paddington (and now site of the Eurostar depot) and was amazed

to find that some of the fittings which supported the trolleybus overhead were still in place.

Then there are the vehicles themselves. In 2005 there are only three places in the UK where trolleybuses can still be operated — the aforementioned Carlton Colville, near Lowestoft, the Black Country Museum at Dudley in the West Midlands and the National Trolleybus Museum at Sandtoft, near Doncaster. Aside from 'Diddler' No 1, London Transport added a 'K1' (1253) and a 'Q1' (No 1768) to its splendid collection of trams, buses and coaches. The original intention had been to add 'C2' No 260, but it was discovered that this had been quite heavily rebuilt in postwar days, and therefore the more original 'K1' was substituted. No 260 might well have been broken up but for the intervention of Tony Belton and the London Trolleybus Preservation Society, who raised the money to buy it from Cohen's and collected it from Clapham Museum in August 1962. In the late 1960s there were still several systems in operation; on 8 October 1967 No 260 was taken on a tour of the Reading system, and on 23 June 1968 it ran in Bournemouth.

A letter from one C. F. Isgar in the April 1968 issue of *Buses* raised the matter of the large number of preserved trolleybus groups then in existence, the problems of co-ordination and, above all, how could the vehicles ever be run again on a regular basis. He cited Crich, which was by then on its way to

Above: A trio of 'L3s' at Fulwell, 26 October 1961. *Author*

becoming the remarkable National Tramway Museum, where today a wonderful selection of restored trams can be enjoyed.

Later a second 'Q1', No 1812, was repatriated from Spain, and following extensive restoration this can be seen in pristine condition carrying passengers at Sandtoft. Along with 'L3' No 1521, 'K1' No 1201 and 'C2' No 260 can both be found at work at Carlton Colville. Two other 'Ks' exist — 'K1' 1253, which as already mentioned is part of the London Transport collection and can be seen at Covent Garden, and 'K2' No 1348, which emigrated to Ireland and joined the National Collection there. The latter was kept at Castleruddery, deep in the Wicklow countryside — sometimes, because of a lack of covered accommodation, out in the open, which did not do it a lot of good — but negotiations are in progress to bring it to Sandtoft and restore it to running order. Finally there is 'H1' No 796, another exile, but this time kept under cover in the Paris Transport Museum, although unfortunately this is not presently open to the public. Given the difficulties of preserving a trolleybus and providing it with the ancillary equipment to enable it to run under its own power, the grand total of nine London examples is a fitting tribute to all those who have helped achieve this.

Left: The end came on the night of 8/9 May 1962. Here a huge crowd welcomes what was officially the last London trolleybus, 'L3' No 1521, as it enters Fulwell depot. Today one may ride on No 1521 at the East Anglia Transport Museum at Carlton Colville, near Lowestoft. *London's Transport Museum*

Right: The driver, 70-year-old Albert West, and conductor, Ronald Gadsby, of No 1521 shake hands at the end of the last journey. *London's Transport Museum*

Lower right: After ending its days with London Transport at Isleworth on 8 May 1962 'K1' No 1348 was shipped across the Irish Sea for preservation at the Irish National Transport Museum. For many years this, operating on a shoestring budget, had to keep many of its exhibits in a field deep in the countryside at Castleruddery in County Wicklow. The 'K1' looks just about as miserable as its companion. It is hoped to bring No 1348 back to the UK for restoration to working order. *Author*

Below: Another London trolleybus to find a home in a foreign museum was Edmonton's 'H1' No 796, which went to Paris, where a transport museum was established in a former bus garage at St Mande. It is seen here alongside one of the legendary and even longer-lived Paris TN6 Renaults, with another London exile, in the shape of a roofbox RT, and (beyond the railings) one of the rare Paris double-deckers (Impériales). Sadly, although the exhibits are perfectly safe, it is several years since they have been accessible to the public. *Author*

· 3 ·

The Met Marches On

SOME rather extraordinary anachronisms began to disappear from the Underground network in 1960. This was the 'T' stock, which had begun life as 'MWs'. Neither appellation sounds particularly exciting, but I expect you would like to know what they stood for. 'M' meant Metropolitan, 'W' was for Westinghouse, which supplied the control equipment, whilst 'T' was simply the next available letter in the alphabet when they were reclassified *c*1940. The designation given by London Transport to its buses and trains has provided a rich source of sometimes quite heated discussion amongst enthusiasts and in learned magazines over the years, but we'll steer clear of that particular minefield. All Underground and

Below: A train of Metropolitan Line 'T' stock, the 9.48am Aldgate–Watford, at Farringdon on 16 June 1962. *Leslie Sandler*

Tube stock had for many years been designed to take into account that most passengers made very short journeys, and therefore ease of entry and exit and plenty of standing room were the greatest priorities. However, the Metropolitan Line out into what the company somewhat brazenly (but very effectively) called Metroland — beyond Harrow to Rickmansworth, Amersham, Chesham, Aylesbury and the Chilterns — was much more like a main line. It shared its tracks with the former Great Central Railway expresses between Marylebone, the Midlands and the North of England; indeed, there had once been plans for it to form part of a through route down to the Kent Coast, under the Channel and on to just about everywhere from Paris to Baghdad and Vladivostok. It never did — well, it hasn't yet — become possible to travel from Chorley Wood or Northwood Hills to such exotic destinations, although

Above: One of the first 10 Metropolitan Line 'T'-stock motor coaches, at Rickmansworth. The last of these trains were withdrawn in 1962, taking the brown livery with them. *G. M. Kichenside*

Right: One of the now-preserved Metropolitan Railway 'MW'-stock compartment-type carriages, its distinctive curved-top doors prominent. *Author*

the creation of the new Channel Tunnel terminus at St Pancras and its connections has opened up some intriguing possibilities.

The trains which operated on the Metropolitan were formed of the sort of carriages you could find working stopping trains on any part of the main-line network and in 1960 were still quite likely to be steam-hauled. Known as 'Dreadnoughts', on account of their impressive appearance (practically anything which moved and was large seems to have been named after the battleship of the same name in

Edwardian times), they were elliptical-roofed, wooden-bodied, 54ft-long compartment vehicles. Painted brown with plenty of lining-out and the impressive Metropolitan Railway coat of arms at each end, they were handsome vehicles and were said to be a response to the equally impressive Great Central Railway carriages with which they competed in the pleasant, affluent, still very green hinterland of the Chilterns.

The last of the original 'Dreadnoughts' came out in 1923, but this was not the end. In the mid-1920s

Above: One of the final Metropolitan 'brown' vehicles, driving trailer No 6735 of 1932. *G. M. Kichenside*

Right: Three Metropolitan Line 'A'-stock trains and two Bakerloo Line 1938-stock Tube trains north of Neasden. In the distance are the chimneys of the soon-to-be-demolished Neasden power station, built in 1905 by the Metropolitan Railway. *Ian Allan Library*

electrification was extended to Rickmansworth and the Watford branch was opened, so more carriages were needed. Open-style vehicles like those on the rest of the Underground network might well have been provided, but it was considered that the patrons of Metroland preferred the seclusion of compartment stock, so more, of a very similar design, were built between 1927 and 1931. In London Transport days both the lining (inevitably but rather sadly) and (equally inevitably) the coat of arms disappeared, but the brown livery, now plain and rather sombre, was retained. Thus it was that when the 1960s opened both multiple-unit and locomotive-hauled versions of such carriages, the oldest dating back to before World War 1, were a common sight at Baker Street and all points north to Aylesbury.

Various replacement options had been considered over a lengthy period of time — indeed, back to the 1930s. One which did go into experimental service, in 1946, was car No 17000. Like Bulleid's contemporary 'Tavern cars' on the Southern, it committed the cardinal sin of ignoring the fact that every passenger likes a corner window seat, if at all possible. It isn't, of course, on a crowded train. But the principle still applies, and No 17000, with a corridor down the length of one side and not many window seats on the other, was doomed to a very short life in this form — three years, to be precise. It was taken back to Acton Works and, as though deeply ashamed of its previous

sins, when it re-emerged it had a new identity, No 17001. Now it had a centre corridor and transverse seating in twos and threes. This was much better, and it formed the prototype for the production vehicles. These were designated 'A' stock, highly appropriate and nothing that anyone could argue about; not only does 'A' stand for Amersham, but practically all the letters of the alphabet had been used up, and it was time to return to the beginning. Cravens of Sheffield, an experienced rolling-stock builder, was given the order in 1959 for 248 'A'-stock carriages. However, unlike the highly distinctive and non-standard bodies of the Craven RTs, the design was just as London Transport stipulated. A further order, for another 216 cars, enabled the 'A' stock to take over Uxbridge-line services.

The 'A' stock was not universally popular, for although as wide as the loading gauge permitted (9ft 8in), an eight-coach train seated only 464 passengers, against 600 in a 'T'-stock train of similar

length. Nevertheless, the new trains came into their own during rush hour, for they could carry many more standing passengers — not that this could be described as 'in comfort', but anyone who has had to stand in a packed compartment carriage will know this is infinitely worse. Of neat if rather bland appearance, the 'A' stock was, like all contemporary Underground and Tube carriages, unpainted save for the roofs, which were grey, although some were originally black. The unpainted alloy sheet panelling did not weather terribly well, and when refurbishment came, decades later, carefully applied areas of red paint did wonders for the 'As'. They have certainly stood the test of time, for in 2005 these units are still with us, the oldest on the Underground network.

The four-tracking to Watford South Junction was completed in 1960 and permitted a vastly improved service — quite the best ever on the Metropolitan.

Below: A 1963 picture of Ruislip station, with an eastbound Piccadilly Line train of 1959 stock at the near platform and an Uxbridge-bound Metropolitan line 'A'-stock train alongside. *C.R.L. Coles*

Electric trains took over operation on the Chesham branch on 12 September 1960, at the same time appearing on the Amersham line, although steam continued north of Rickmansworth for another year. By this time the former Great Central route, which had passed into LNER ownership in 1923, had, under British Railways, eventually moved from Eastern to London Midland Region control. The not-very-wonderful Thompson 'L1' 2-6-4Ts which in the mid-1950s had taken over suburban services from the rather better Robinson 4-6-2Ts were in turn ousted by LMS and BR Standard 2-6-4Ts, whilst LMS-type 2-6-2Ts worked the Chesham branch. These latter hauled a set of really ancient, low-roofed carriages, dating from 1898-1900 and known as 'Ashburys', after their builder. These could never make up their minds whether they wanted to be steam trains or electrics. They had started out as the former, being converted to EMUs and then back to steam-hauled stock in London Transport days. They were not finished, even in 1960, for several passed into preservation on the Bluebell Railway, to be hauled for ever and a day by steam engines — one hopes! It had been decided not to electrify north of Amersham, so

Above: A Chesham-branch train consisting of 1898 Ashbury stock propelled by LMS-type 2-6-2T No 41284 heads away from the Aylesbury line on 11 September 1960, the last full day of steam working. *C. R. L. Coles*

Right: In the Dickensian depths of the City of London near Farringdon a train of late-1930s Metadyne stock heads towards King's Cross. To the right are the British Railways tracks leading to Moorgate. *Ian Allan Library*

when, in September 1961, steam and the 'T' stock finally ceased operating, British Rail took over all services to Aylesbury, using DMUs. As well as the Marylebone route it was (and is) possible to reach Aylesbury by the former GWR line from Princes Risborough. Steam could still be seen for a little while longer on the through trains out of Marylebone, latterly in the charge of grubby, run-down Stanier '5MTs', but the service itself was doomed, and trains ceased to run north of Aylesbury in September 1966. However, the track through Quainton Road and on to the junction with the Oxford–Bletchley line remained, and shortly a preservation site would open at Quainton which would achieve wonders, not least in the preservation of various items of London Transport rolling stock.

Upper left: A District Line train of Metadyne stock climbs into the daylight at Ravenscourt Park. *Author*

Above: Ealing Common District Line depot, June 1969. *Ian Allan Library*

Upper right: Uxbridge station, with its dramatic reinforced concrete roof. On the left is a Piccadilly Line train of pre-1938 stock, on the right a District Line train of Metadyne stock. *Ian Allan Library*

Lower left: New Cross East London Line depot, 4 August 1963. The furthest train is headed by a clerestory-roofed 'G'-stock car, built by the Gloucester Railway Carriage & Wagon Co in 1923, the other two being composed of highly distinctive 'F'-stock all-steel cars, known as 'Tanks', built in 1920 by the Metropolitan Carriage, Wagon & Finance Co of Birmingham. London Transport certainly got its money's worth out of these long-lived veterans. *Leslie Sandler*

Lower right: District Line 'G'-class clerestory-roofed driving car of 1923 at Parsons Green on 30 December 1960, heading a train bound for Putney Bridge. *Author's collection*

· 4 ·

One Hundred Years of the Met — and Other Celebrations

IN 1963 the Metropolitan Railway celebrated its centenary. The 1960s was an era when recognition of the enormous part played by all forms of transport in the history of the UK, particularly since the Industrial Revolution, took on a different dimension. No longer the preserve of enthusiasts and specialist historians, it was seen as woven into the very fabric of everyone's lives, even those who scorned the use of all forms of public transport, whatever the cost to society, and, building on the work of dedicated enthusiasts, events took place throughout the decade celebrating our rich and diverse transport history. Many preservation groups and museums came into being, often with little more than boundless enthusiasm and optimism to get them started. Today most survive, now long-established, highly professional and perhaps taken for granted — which should never be so.

David Kaye, in his *Veteran and Vintage Public Service Vehicles* (published by Ian Allan in 1962), wrote: 'It is unfortunately only in the last few years that the need to preserve old buses, coaches and trams has become realised.' He went on to list the numbers of preserved PSVs, coming up with 'at least 32 Leylands and 17 AECs' but noting that 'only one Daimler, one Guy and no Karriers are left'. The most recent dated from 1948, which would have been the London 'Q1' trolleybus, No 1768. In the 2002 edition of the PSV Circle's *Preserved Buses* there are 164 pages of lists of

vehicles, each page listing some 35 vehicles, which comes to a total of around 5,740 buses, coaches, trolleybuses and trams. Not the least surprising aspect of this extraordinary total is that there are infinitely more than the 32 Leylands and 17 AECs which had already ceased work in 1962. What this means is that, apart from a few which David Kaye inevitably missed, there is a huge number which would then have been lying about in scrapyards, at the back of garages, in fields, converted to showmen's vehicles, dumped in all manner of places and considered beyond redemption but which have since been either brought back to life or are at least saved in various states of restoration.

London Transport had long been a pioneer in the preservation field, and in 1963 it staged a Metropolitan Railway centenary parade at Neasden. Among the locomotives displayed were No 23, the very last of the famous 4-4-0Ts dating from 1866 which powered Underground trains in steam days and which had been returned to its 1903 open-cab condition, and No L44, an 'E'-class 0-4-4T of 1898, which had once been Metropolitan Railway No 1. The 0-4-4T headed a rake of 'Ashbury' carriages. All would survive, the carriages on the Bluebell Railway, whilst the locomotive is now on display in London's Transport Museum at Covent Garden. As for No 1, I had the great pleasure of riding behind it at Quainton last year (2004), having travelled there from Covent Garden in RT4712 of the London Transport collection, decked out in the gold livery applied two years earlier for HM the Queen's Golden Jubilee celebrations. Bliss indeed.

Before the 1960s were out RTs would be entering preservation, the very first in the UK being one of the 'prewar' examples, RT113, which became the property of the 2RT2 group on 1 May 1963, having been bought from London Transport for the sum of £105, although even before this an RT8 had gone to a museum in St Louis in the USA in 1961. This latter was more or less the beginning of what became a veritable flood of British double-deckers taking up

Upper right: No 23, one of the original Metropolitan Railway 'A'-class 4-4-0Ts rebuilt with a cab, seen in London Transport days heading an engineers' train near Wembley. *Ian Allan Library*

Lower right: The now-preserved No 23, the undoubted star of the Metropolitan Centenary celebrations, passing the viewing stands on 23 May 1963 coupled to 'a four-car set of aluminium-alloy 'A' stock, the Metropolitan's latest type of car', to quote contemporary publicity. This might have been the Swinging 'Sixties, but London Transport officials had not yet entirely forsaken the trilby and bowler hat. *London Transport*

residence across the Atlantic. Not all were ex-London, but such is the perceived attraction of the red double-decker that I was hardly surprised on my first visit to California to come across a former Wilts & Dorset Bristol Lodekka (which had once regularly passed down my road on its way from Poole to Swanage) heading down Fisherman's Walk in Monterey, apparently on its way to Piccadilly via Trafalgar Square.

With the end of locomotive-hauled passenger trains on the Metropolitan the Bo-Bo electric locomotives were now redundant. There was still a need for steam, and one-time Great Western Railway

Upper left: A former Great Western Railway '57xx' pannier tank at Neasden in 1969. *Author*

Lower left: Wembley Park flyover, with Metropolitan-Vickers Bo-Bo electric locomotive No 8 heading for Baker Street. *London Transport*

Below: Neasden depot in 1969. Beyond the sidings full of Metropolitan Line 'A' stock and Bakerloo Line 1938 stock a former GWR pannier tank is dwarfed by the power station in course of demolition. *Author*

pannier tanks continued in Engineer's Department service throughout the 1960s. The very last train of traditional 'Dreadnought' compartment stock was a special to Aylesbury on 26 May 1963, hauled as far as Amersham by Bo-Bo No 5 *John Hampden*. An unlikely home for one 'Dreadnought' was the Keighley & Worth Valley Railway in Yorkshire, where it found itself trundling up and down past woollen mills deep in the Pennines — a landscape somewhat different from the gentle Chilterns and art-deco semi-detacheds. Two of the final batch of compartment carriages of 1932, Nos 2758 and 2749, lived on at Neasden, converted to a sleet unit to clear the track in icy winter conditions and numbered ESL118A and ESL118B.

Four of the electric locomotives lasted for some time beyond 1963, in the service department, one (No 3) being scrapped in 1965, another (No 1) going in 1974. The final two were preserved: No 5 *John Hampden* can be seen at Covent Garden, whilst, most excitingly, No 12 *Sarah Siddons* experienced a whole new lease of life, working enthusiasts' specials, not just over the Underground network but also on various parts of the Southern Electric system.

Upper left: The two 1932-built 'T'-stock carriages, Nos 2758/49, converted to a double-unit sleet locomotive Nos ESL118A/ESL118B, at Neasden in 1969. *Author*

Lower left: The preserved former Metropolitan Railway Bo-Bo electric locomotive *Sarah Siddons* during a 'Steam on the Met' event in the 1990s. *Author*

Right: One of the preserved Metropolitan Railway carriages, built by Ashburys in 1898, converted to push-pull configuration in 1940 to work between Rickmansworth and Chesham and now preserved on the Bluebell Railway. *Author*

Below: The preserved former Metropolitan Railway 'E'-class 0-4-4T No 1. *Author*

• 5 •

Upward and Onward Down in the Tube

ON 19 November 1960 three eight-car trains of 1960 prototype Tube stock entered service on the Central Line. Intended to be the next generation, in the event they remained unique, although certain features were incorporated into the Victoria Line trains, ordered in 1964 and delivered from September 1967. We'll come back to these, but first the 1960 vehicles. There were only 12 actual new carriages, all driving motor cars, built by Cravens, the rest being 12 elderly trailers dating from 1927 and 1931. New Wedglock automatic couplers and what was in effect double-glazing were the chief new features. Inevitably the trailer cars were destined for early withdrawal, and the genuine 1960 cars were to have fairly chequered if useful careers, being used as guinea pigs for a number of experiments. Four were scrapped in the 1980s, the rest later.

The reason so few 1960s carriages were built was that new stock was needed urgently on the Central Line at the beginning of the 1960s and so, unable to wait for trials of new vehicles to be satisfactorily completed, more 1959 stock, based on the 1956 prototypes, was ordered. The first 1959 train only just managed to enter service in the year from which it took its name, 11 days before Christmas 1959, taking up work on the Piccadilly Line. It was followed by 75 more trains, each of seven vehicles. Ultimately there were 532 carriages of 1959 stock at work on the Piccadilly Line and 57 on the Central Line, all built by Metro-Cammell. Their successors were known as the 1962 stock, the first beginning work on the Central Line in April 1962. There were even more of these, 646 in all, 470 built by Metro-Cammell, and 176 by British Rail at its Derby Works. Despite being given a separate designation the 1962 stock was to all intents and purposes identical to the 1959, although through the 1960s the 1959 trains worked the Piccadilly Line, and the 1962 stock the Central, with one three-car train of 1962 stock working the Holborn–Aldwych shuttle service.

The 1959 and 1962 stock bore a distinct family resemblance to the 1938 stock, especially when seen from the side, but the front had a more upright appearance, with vents either side of the destination indicator, which was placed above the front windows rather than below. The five marker lights of the 1938 stock had disappeared, as headcodes were no longer used. Internally the layout was also similar to that of

Left: 1959 stock at Holborn, shortly after taking over this shuttle service from the pre-1938 stock. *Kenneth Harris*

Upper right: A 1959-stock Central Line train pulls out of North Weald for Ongar past the only semaphore signals on the LT network. This was once LNER (and formerly Great Eastern Railway) territory. *John Glover*

Lower right: 1962 stock at home . *Ian Allan Library*

Above: A pre-1938 Piccadilly Line train at Aldwych, which branch would close in the 1990s. *Ian Allan Library*

Below: 1959 stock stands outside the southernmost extremity of the Tube network at Morden depot. *Author*

the 1938 stock; the main colour was blue instead of green, and fluorescent lighting now made an appearance, but there was still plenty of varnished wood. Externally, London Transport persisted with the rather dull unpainted aluminium finish.

Delivery of the 1962 stock allowed the withdrawal of all the pre-1938 units — in other words everything not built by London Transport. However, 43 of these vintage vehicles had a most surprising reprieve. By the spring of 1966 the railways of the Isle of Wight had been reduced to the 8½-mile Ryde Pier Head–Shanklin section; British Rail would have liked to be rid of this too, but instead it was authorised to electrify the line. The Island's lines had always been subject to severe loading-gauge restrictions, which meant that everything — locomotives, carriages and wagons — dated from pre-Grouping days, so that by 1966 there was at work nothing built later than 1923. When the Island was offered some very slightly newer Tube trains it had little choice but to accept.

The chosen vehicles were overhauled at Acton Works, being converted for third-rail electrification, and were then hauled to Stewarts Lane depot, Battersea, where they underwent some internal modifications and were repainted in Rail blue, finally beginning work on the Island in March 1967.

With a few exceptions — vehicles damaged in accidents — the 1938 stock continued to work right through the 1960s, scrapping on a large scale beginning only in 1972.

On 20 August 1962 London Transport gained Government approval for construction of the Victoria Line, the first all-new Tube line for decades, although plans for it went back to the 1940s. The first section, from Walthamstow to Highbury & Islington, opened in September 1968. The line itself and the trains which operated it marked a quantum leap forward, much greater than that of any other postwar Underground development. We will examine this in some detail in a later chapter.

Above: Two pre-1938 trains after transfer to the Isle of Wight, seen at Ryde St Johns. That on the left is just leaving for Shanklin and is passing the semaphore signal controlled by the former South Eastern & Chatham Railway 'box, also transferred from the mainland. The train on the right is standing outside the works. *Author*

Right: More semaphore signals between the tunnels at the approach to King's Cross main-line station. A train of 1938 Tube stock topped and tailed by battery locomotives (that nearer the camera built by the Gloucester Railway Carriage & Wagon Co, also in 1938) passes a British Rail Brush Type 4 (Class 47) which has just brought in an express from Edinburgh, whilst in the distance an English Electric Type 4 (Class 40) is emerging with another up train. *Author*

6

The Routemaster Rolls On

JUST as production of the RT family barely slackened after London's last trams had been replaced, so 10 years later Routemaster production continued after the last Isleworth- and Fulwell-based trolleybus routes had succumbed to the motor bus. However, there seemed to be no hurry, for 1962 would almost be out before RMs began to replace the RT family on Central Area routes. However, they then arrived with a vengeance — a Christmas present for passengers on routes 73, 13 and 16. Some 156 Routemasters replaced an equal number of RTLs and RTs, which was interesting given the greater capacity of the new bus and was contrary to the original intention of the policy makers that nine RMs should replace every 10 RTs/RTLs.

Of what then seemed of even greater import, and certainly attracting greater publicity, was the entry into Green Line service of the production Routemaster coaches (RMCs). On 29 August 18 of these impressive-looking vehicles took up work from Hertford and Guildford garages on the 715 and 715A routes, replacing RF single-deckers. Attracting publicity was one thing, but attracting passengers was quite another, and, excellent though the double-deck coaches eventually proved to be, various factors told against them. Frequency was reduced from every 20 minutes to half-hourly, competing diesel and electric trains replacing steam proved attractive to both commuters and shoppers, and more and more people were turning to the car for their regular transport. Front and rear suspensions caused problems, and the brakes were not entirely reliable. By December 1962 some 68 RMCs (plus the 1957 prototype) were at work on routes serving the new towns.

It would be tedious to list all the routes which were converted to Routemaster operation as the decade progressed — this information can be found elsewhere — but we will note some highlights. Routemaster production through the mid-1960s was much slower than was that of the RT family at its height, when not only RTs but also RTLs and RTWs were entering service, as well as the lowbridge provincial-style RLHs and stopgap SRTs. Essentially it was the busiest Central London routes which received Routemasters, although inevitably they turned up elsewhere, especially at weekends. At first it continued to be RTs and especially RTLs which were

Left: RM249, one of the early trolleybus-replacement Routemasters with original radiator and non-opening front upper-deck windows, working from Poplar depot at Shoreditch, 20 August 1966. *Gerald Mead*

Above: Fulwell's RM1068 at Heathrow Airport, on a route which replaced trolleybus route 605 on 9 May 1962 (not that trolleybuses ever reached Heathrow). *Ian Allan Library*

Below: RMs 584 and 514 at the Highgate Village terminus of the 271, a few weeks after motor buses took over from the 611 trolleybus route, which disappeared on 19 July 1960. *Author*

Above: Surrounded by high-rise office buildings under construction in the City of London, RM939 heads southwards on route 141 (replacing trolleybus 641) on 18 November 1961. *W. H. R. Godwin*

Left: The unpainted Routemaster, RM664, working from Highgate garage on trolleybus-replacement (and extended) route 127 in Whitehall, 14 October 1961. *Gerald Mead*

Upper left: Green Line RMC1459 at Cheshunt on its way south to Guildford, August 1962. *Ian Allan Library*

Above: Green Line RMC1470 turns out of Baker Street on its way to Wrotham in 1965. *Author*

Left: The one prototype Routemaster which was kept working in normal passenger service throughout the 1960s was RMC4, seen here heading for Bishops Stortford. *Author's collection*

Above: Clapham Common, with an RM and a Green Line RF negotiating the traffic. Just out of sight beyond the RM is the Museum of British Transport, situated in the former Clapham bus garage.
Author's collection

Right: RM794 at Trafalgar Square on night route N83.
Capital Transport

Above: Minister of Transport Ernest Marples takes charge of RM831 on the famous Chiswick Works skid pan, 15 June 1961. RTs were normally employed on this duty throughout the 1960s and into the '70s. *Ian Allan Library*

replaced, but in October 1962 the 8ft-wide RTW class began its retreat when Routemasters moved into Putney (AF) garage to work the 74.

The 74 was one of the routes that my generation, which grew up during World War 2, always associated with the 'prewar' RTs. These had long since departed from Central Area passenger service, but 61 were still in stock at the beginning of 1963, having spent years as trainers. All but three were sold that year. At the very beginning of 1963 I came across RT79, one of the seven repainted green in 1955 and destined to be the last still in use as a trainer, parked, rather appropriately, at Dunton Green, below the North Downs; it was delicensed in February and sold for scrap. Two others lasted out of use until 1964, but this wasn't quite the end of the type, for there was still one very special bus in London Transport possession. This was 1037J, a mobile instruction unit. The chassis was that of postwar Cravens RT1420, which had lost its body

Above: Withdrawal of the lowbridge RLH class began in 1964. RLH23 stands at the Upminster Station terminus of the 248, a one-time single-deck route which the class took over in 1955. *A. M. Wright*

Above: Upton Park's RTW60 stands at the Barking terminus of route 100, 5 August 1962. Routemasters would take over on route 100 at the end of 1964. *Gerald Mead*

Below: Camberwell's RT2211 surrounded by Routemasters at Aldgate *c*1969. *J. G. S. Smith*

following an argument with a low bridge in 1954. Its replacement was none other than the prototype RT body, the daddy of them all, completed in the spring of 1939 and mounted on the prototype chassis which had been running experimentally under an elderly open-staircase body as ST1140 but which now became RT1. Because of its more modern chassis 1037J largely escaped the attention of enthusiasts throughout the 1960s, although one group, the 2RT2 Preservation Group, kept its eye on it. It remained London Transport property until as late as 1978, when it was bought by the late Prince Marshall, reappearing — to great surprise and an ecstatic welcome — as RT1 in the cavalcade marking the very last day of RT service, from Barking garage on 7 April 1979.

Above: 'Prewar' RT90 (actually delivered in 1940) heads a line of driver-training vehicles leaving Chiswick Works in April 1962.
M. C. Beamish

Left: Dunton Green garage, last refuge for the 'prewar' RT trainer, was also home to No 970J, a former Country Area forward-entrance STL (1039) converted to a tree-lopper. It was replaced in 1962 by a Thames Trader. *Author*

7

The Last Routemasters Enter Service

BY the late 1950s the Routemaster, although not yet in normal service, was already in some respects out of step with what was happening elsewhere in the UK. Leyland's rear-engined Atlantean was several steps ahead, and if not as reliable, pointed the way forward, in terms of both layout and capacity. Of course, the Routemaster's extraordinary longevity and the unique operating conditions in Central London would eventually tell in its favour, but what could not be denied was that it was a rather small bus; even with a conductor you needed as great a capacity as possible to get the economics right. So in the summer of 1961 a stretched Routemaster had appeared, taking up work in November and replacing the 70-seat trolleybuses which had hitherto worked from Finchley depot on route 609.

The stretching was done very simply, by inserting a 2ft 4in bay amidships, enabling an additional row of seats to be added upstairs and down, increasing capacity to 72. The original classification of ER (extended Routemaster) was changed almost immediately to RML (Routemaster lengthened). Initially there were 24 of them, RML880-903. They had the same size engines as the shorter RM but this proved perfectly able to cope with the additional weight. One might wonder why production didn't instantly switch to the RML. One reason was London Transport's innate conservatism — in some areas — and another was union concern that a fleet of larger buses would mean rather fewer in total and therefore crew redundancies. Events, not least recruitment difficulties in these increasingly affluent times, rapidly overtook such considerations and, belatedly, the RML became standard, the first of the later examples being RML2261, which became London Transport property in July 1965.

Based on the RML but delivered ahead of the main batch, in the spring and summer of 1965, were a further 43 Green Line coaches, RCL2218-60. This

Right: RML2303 at AEC's Southall works on 14 September 1965, before delivery to London Transport. *Ian Allan Library*

Above: The RCL class of 43 30ft Green Line coaches surely represented the peak of the Routemaster design. RCL2220 was one of 28 to displace RTs from Romford garage on routes 721, 722 and 726 in June 1965. *Gerald Mead*

might seem perverse, given that one-man operation was just over the horizon, but these longer-wheelbase versions were destined to upgrade routes which were already worked by double-deckers, namely those based at Romford and Grays. STLs, wartime D-class Daimlers and, for the last 15 years, RTs had operated the intensive East London 721, 722, 723 and 726 routes, and in June 1965 the 65-seat RCLs took over. Less plagued by initial problems than were the RMCs, the RCLs represented the zenith of the Routemaster design, although they were to have very little opportunity to display their qualities exactly as had been planned.

The first route to receive the later RMLs was the Country Area's 409 from West Croydon to Forest Row, on the edge of the Ashdown Forest in Sussex and the most southerly point reached by London Transport buses. Until now there had been no green Routemaster buses (as opposed to Green Line coaches), and even now most of those which were sent to Godstone garage were actually red, pending delivery of sufficient green examples, thus reversing the situation of some 16 years earlier, when brand-new green-painted RTs briefly worked in Central London from Middle Row and Mortlake garages. The RMLs began work with effect from 3 October

1965, 17 being red, 11 green; East Grinstead and Reigate also had a single green RML each. The red buses soon took themselves off to Tottenham, where trials were to begin in comparison with Atlanteans, or Stamford Hill, so that the Country Area once again became all-green. By this time the practice of borrowing red buses at weekends to supplement services had died out, as fewer and fewer people used public transport for pleasure trips out to the countryside. Much as I loved a ride sitting on the upstairs front seat of a double-decker, nothing compared with our first family outing by car when private motoring resumed after the War; this was to Reigate Heath, where we had a picnic and watched lowbridge Godstone STLs heading along the A25 and also inspected a nearly new Southdown Park Royal-bodied Leyland Tiger PS1 on an afternoon excursion from the coast. By the start of the 1960s the STLs had long since been succeeded by RLHs, but in 1965 these too disappeared from the 410, being replaced by RMLs from Godstone, the route having been diverted to avoid the offending railway bridge in Oxted. One wonders why this hadn't happened years earlier.

More Routemaster buses entered Country Area service at Northfleet later in 1965, at High Wycombe in February 1966, at Garston and Hemel Hempstead in March of that year, and, finally, completing the grand total of 100 green RMLs, at Windsor and Harlow in May. Although their days in green livery

Above: Immediately after the RCLs came the 500 production RMLs, 400 of which were for the Central Area. RML2295, seen in East Road near Old Street, spent its first few weeks as a temporary Country Area bus before transferring to Tottenham garage in November 1965.
Gerald Mead

Upper left: RLH22 of Godstone outside Reigate garage, about to set off for Bromley. By 1965 RMLs would replace the RLHs on the 410. *F. G. Reynolds*

Lower left: The rear aspect of the Country Area RML is shown by RML2306 in Kentish countryside, heading for Bromley North station. *John B. Gaff*

Above: Red RML2301, temporarily allocated to Godstone garage, at Redhill, 10 October 1965. *Gerald Mead*

Below: Where once trams and trolleybuses met, an RM and an RT — to say nothing of a Morris Oxford estate and a Vauxhall Victor — negotiate Tooting Broadway. *Ian Allan Library*

would be cut short, the great majority would serve London for over 30 years, being bought back by London Transport and repainted red in the late 1970s.

New red Routemasters went to Putney, Stockwell, Upton Park, Hackney, and Willesden in 1966, to Holloway, Riverside, Uxbridge, Hanwell and Croydon in 1967. There was also a good deal of shuffling around of existing Routemasters, both short and long versions. The year 1968 opened with production almost at an end. Croydon received most of the final few, for the 130 series of routes serving New Addington — or Little Siberia, as the vast, windswept estate on top of the North Downs was known to its sometimes reluctant inhabitants. The very last, RML2760, went to Upton Park. All started work on 1 March. However, the last RML actually to enter London Transport service was RML2548, which settled at Chalk Farm on 30 May 1968 after completing an overseas tour.

Two further Routemaster variations appeared in 1966. The more notable was FRM1; this was a rear-engined bus but contained 60% standard Routemaster parts and seated 72 passengers in its front-entrance Park Royal body. It remained unique. Used experimentally on various routes, including one-man operation from Croydon garage on the 233 (just within our time frame, from December 1969), it had come too late. A changing world, including spiralling labour costs, which were making bus and coach production in the London area less and less viable, the inevitable teething problems afflicting any proto-type, and the availability of the off-the-peg rear-engined buses, meant that it remained unique. It became part of the London Transport Museum collection in 1984 and as I write can usually be seen on open days at the Museum Depot at Acton.

The other Routemaster variation of 1966 — rather more successful, in as much as it did go into limited production — was developed from RMF1254, an otherwise standard front-engined half-cab bus which had been built to a length of 30ft and fitted with a forward entrance. Between October 1962 and mid-1963 it was sent off around the country to try to drum up orders for AEC. Northern General bought 50, while 65 shorter (27ft 6in) versions were ordered by British European Airways in 1966 to replace its $1\frac{1}{2}$-deck AEC Regal IV coaches. The BEA examples towed passengers' luggage in trailers and, like their predecessors, were operated by London Transport on behalf of the airline, being painted in BEA colours. RMF1254 itself never ran in service for London Transport, and following a spell on loan to BEA was sold to work with similar buses in the North East. In the 1970s all BEA's own vehicles would pass to London Transport, some working briefly in passenger service from North Street, Romford, others becoming trainers and staff buses, and would generally have a very varied post-airline career.

Above: The solitary rear-engined Routemaster, FRM1, comes off the flyover crossing South End, Croydon, both bus and road being 1960s developments. *Author*

Below: The impressively neat rear end of FRM1. The bus is pictured on route 233, which — despite the fact that Roundshaw Estate was built on part of the old Croydon (once London) Airport —was hardly the most prestigious use for this distinguished vehicle. *Author*

Above: RMF1254 on the Park Royal stand at the 1962 Commercial Motor Show at Earl's Court. This forward-entrance bus would never enter passenger service with London Transport, eventually migrating to Tyneside, to join the Northern General fleet. *Ian Allan Library*

Upper right: RMF1254's experimental use on British European Airways' service from Kensington to Heathrow led to the building of a batch of similar buses to replace the airline's RF-derived 1½-deck coaches. It is seen in January 1964 complete with trailer. *Ian Allan Library*

Lower right: The first of the British European Airways forward-entrance Routemasters, KGJ 601D, at the airline's West London Air Terminal at Gloucester Road, Kensington. On the right of the picture is one of the previous generation of BEA airport coaches — AEC Regal IVs with 1½-deck bodywork by Park Royal. *Ian Allan Library*

• 8 •

Country and Green Line Matters

Left: Roofbox RT4268 of Hemel Hempstead (HH) garage at the Warners End terminus of the 314A, 14 September 1963. This variety of RT disappeared from the Country Area at the end of January 1964. *Gerald Mead*

BY the mid-1960s the future of London Transport's Country Area and the Green Line network was being discussed at many levels, and a consensus was emerging that the status quo could not continue. In the Winter 1966/7 issue of *Country Bus News* there was a pertinent article by B. A. Seaman of Hatfield headed 'Should the GLC Run its Own Bus Services?', which raised a number of points resulting from a Camden borough councillor's suggestion that the GLC should take over London Transport. Whilst agreeing that 'the service as it stands is a poor one', he points out that 'London Transport suffers enormously due to staff shortages and adverse traffic conditions' and that 'coupled with some internal restrictions this all leads to situations that prompt other persons to think they could do better'. He also thinks that the Camden councillor has misunderstood the status of the Country Area,

of which the 29 garages and 6,000 staff operated largely beyond GLC jurisdiction. Seaman quotes a Barnet councillor who proposed a levy on GLC residents towards the higher wages necessary to attract and retain staff and, in relation to the Country Area, adds that 'employers who bring in staff from outside London should pay an amount per person for this contribution to the already congested traffic problem'.

In another article Mr Seaman questions whether the introduction of the 72-seat RML has been a progressive move, given that 'the ratio of change has been about two vehicles for three', which 'can mean a lesser service being fully operated as opposed to a better service suffering cuts in journeys owing to staff shortages'. But this could mean a noticeably poorer service in the Country Area; 'where you had three buses per hour you now have two . . . the poor old passenger comes to the end of his tether and makes

Above: Chelsham *c*1969. On the garage forecourt are RT3130, which will cover a fair slice of rural and suburban Surrey on its way to Dorking, and RT1027 on the local 453, having come up the hill from Caterham. On the far left a Green Line RF prepares to set off for Aylesbury on the 706. *Author*

Right: Interior of a Country Area RF. *Author*

other travelling arrangements'. The fact that during a 15-hour day a double-decker (the 56-seat RT) was 'full up for approximately 30 minutes would suggest a SMALLER bus is adequate . . . a 39-seater single-deck bus would be ample. This could also lead to that same 39-seater bus being one-man operated.' In the same issue there is a picture of one such bus (or, in Green Line parlance, coach), which, 'although this class of vehicle is now 14 years old they [*sic*] are in

sound mechanical and body condition . . . repainted Lincoln Green with a broad pale-green band edged with aluminium beading below the window line . . . newly fitted four headlamp system and the curved windscreen.' This was RF136, the first of a fleet of refurbished RFs which would outlast Routemasters on Green Line service and very nearly on Country Area bus service too.

Moving in a very different direction, Colin Curtis

Right: The Country Area's eight Daimler Fleetlines entered service in September 1965 on route 424 from East Grinstead garage, XF3 being seen in Bell Street, Reigate, in October of that year. *Roy Hobbs*

contributes a piece, alongside a full-page picture, on 'The Daimler Fleetline — Vehicle Code XF'. After noting that 'there is nothing new in the world — only that somebody rediscovers something from the past' and reminding the reader of 'a front-entrance double-deck vehicle produced in 1934, namely Q4' and that 'Q5 followed for Country Area service and, later, Q188 for Green Line duty', he gives technical details of the Country Area's new double-deck design. He goes on to declare that 'from an engineering viewpoint the writer prefers the conventional vehicle with the engine at the forward end' — perhaps not surprising, from one so associated with the Route-master — and concludes: 'We are living through changing times, and time alone will tell whether this will be the principle of the bus for tomorrow.'

Precise figures for the number of passengers using Green Line and Country Bus services are difficult to deduce, as from 1963 onwards these were lumped together, but in 1962 there were two million fewer Green Line passenger journeys than in 1961. The decline matched that of the previous year; had it continued at this rate, before the century was out there would have been no Green Line passengers at all. Things never got quite that bad, but the traditional network, with routes from all points of the compass in the Home Counties passing through Central London and terminating a roughly equal distance in the opposite direction, was doomed. Increasing congestion meant that more and more routes began to terminate in or close to Central London.

There were attempts to prove that the decline need

not be terminal. By cutting out the majority of stops and using sections of the new motorways then opening up on the outskirts of London, certain routes really did become express rather than glorified bus routes. In 1964 the 727 was introduced between Tring, via Hemel Hempstead town centre and 14 miles of the M1 (to Mill Hill), and Victoria. However, various problems, unrelated to the motorway section, militated against its success, and it did not last. Westwards the opening of the M4 enabled Windsor, still a popular Green Line destination, to be reached more quickly, and this proved more successful, although problems with recruitment in the Windsor area did not help. Electrification of the line out of Fenchurch Street and a much better District Line service on the Upminster line right into the West End instead of the Green Line terminus at Aldgate meant that the once heavily used double-deck routes out east could spare some of their Routemasters for transfer to the Windsor services. They hardly became long-term residents there and indeed were leading an increasingly nomadic existence. In 1966 RCLs were sent to Godstone to work all that was left of the once hourly 709, which used to link Chesham with Godstone (a 3hr 10min journey) but now was reduced to two commuter runs into London and back home again; ironically this would prove to be the most permanent Green Line work the Routemasters ever managed to perform, their stay being no less than 10 years. Upon overhaul (from 1967 onwards) the RMCs and RCLs lost their pale-green window surrounds, which modification

Above: The first OMO Green Line route was the 724 (Romford–High Wycombe), upon which RF34 is seen shortly after the route's introduction in 1966. *London Transport*

Left: Deep in the North Downs, GS42 of Dorking (DS) garage stands at the Ranmore terminus of the 433 on a bleak winter's day in 1968. *Mark Chadwick*

did nothing to enhance their appearance. By the end of the decade many of the earlier vehicles had been demoted to bus duties.

One-man operation came to Central London Green Line services in November 1968, on routes 701, 702, 710, 711, 714, 719 and 720, with more following early in 1969. These were preceded by the 724, which orbital route had been introduced in July 1966 to link High Wycombe with Amersham, Watford, St Albans, Welwyn Garden City, Hertford, Harlow and Epping and Romford. It was followed in

May 1967 by another OMO route, the 727 from Crawley to Luton. This served both Gatwick and Heathrow airports and, later, Luton. Although not much remarked upon at the time this would prove to be of enormous significance, for with the huge growth in holiday air travel coach services to the various airports surrounding London would grow at an equal rate.

By the early 1960s the little 26-seat Guys of the GS class were beginning to fade away, and a notable development of 1963 saw three sold to Tillingbourne

Valley Services, which painted them in its maroon livery and set them to work between Guildford and Peaslake on route 448, which was shared with London Transport and upon which they worked alongside London Transport's own examples. In the same year the first members of the RF class were declared surplus to requirements, and 10 of the first batch — RF16-25, originally private-hire coaches but converted to Green Line use in 1956 — were sold. They were followed in 1964 by the other 15 and the big, ECW-bodied RFWs, London Transport's only true coaches, when it was decided to close down the Private Hire Department, partly as a result of competition and partly because the recruiting of staff was becoming more and more difficult.

The year 1965 saw the arrival of the RF's intended replacement, the RC. The class comprised 14 Willowbrook-bodied AEC Reliances; 36ft long and 8ft 2½in wide, these were virtually standard provincial vehicles, their BET-style bodies being similar to those used by Southdown, Maidstone & District and East Kent, mostly on bus work, although the RCs had proper coach-type seats with headrests. A new and rather striking livery of white with Lincoln-green waistband was applied, although this was soon replaced by a more sober, predominantly green version. They were sent initially to Windsor and Dunton Green garages to work the 705, a section of which used the M4 motorway — although other sections involved congested inner London roads and narrow Kent lanes. Like so many vehicle initiatives from now on, good intentions were let down by faulty mechanics. The RCs were scarcely up to the job, breakdowns being frequent; they had been relegated to bus work by the early 1970s and would soon be withdrawn. Nevertheless, further Reliances would be ordered for Green Line work early in the 1970s.

Above: The Private Hire RFs were instantly recognisable by their cant windows. In 1956 10 were transferred to the Green Line fleet, and by 1961 RF23 was working from Garston on route 719. *Author*

Right: In the 1960s the RF class far outnumbered all other London Transport single-deckers. Private Hire RF7, seen at Waterloo on 2 June 1963, was one of the first to be withdrawn. *Gerald Mead*

Above: RFW12, one of the Private Hire fleet of 15 ECW-bodied AEC Regal IVs, at Waterloo in 1963. *Gerald Mead*

Below: One of the Green Line Willowbrook-bodied RC-class Reliances of 1965, seen passing Gatwick Airport on the 727 in the summer of 1969. *Author*

The year 1963 had seen the opening of the much-needed Dartford Tunnel. This was closer to the sea by a good few miles than was the case with any other fixed crossing of the Thames — an indication both of the seeming relentless spread of the London suburbs along the Thames Estuary and also of the move of port facilities away from their traditional home in the Pool of London and the East End.

The story of the decline of what had been the busiest dock system in the world mirrors the changes which were taking place in the world economy and the social changes which these brought about. By the end of the 1960s what had once been a densely populated area heavily dependent upon public transport was changing rapidly, yet by one set of measurements the Port of London reached its peak as late as 1964, when it handled a total tonnage of 61,339,000. However, only four years later, in 1968, the docks nearest Central London, St Katherine's Dock and London Docks, both closed.

The steep decline and annihilation of the entire dock system, its replacement by Docklands (creating a very different society), the soap *EastEnders* and the Docklands Light Railway lay in the future, albeit one which was not so far away.

Bus services were run through the Dartford Tunnel, Country Area RTs operating the 300 between Dartford and Grays, whilst five odd-looking double-deckers (TT1-5), with Strachans bodywork on Thames Trader chassis (presumably because the Ford factory was just up the river) were provided for cyclists and pedestrians. However, the citizens of Kent had never had much to say to Essex men and women and *vice versa*; few saw any reason why a tunnel should alter this situation, the services being under-used and soon abandoned.

The Thames has always divided Londoners into North and South, and at the same time it has done more than anything else to shape the capital. In my childhood perhaps the most eagerly awaited family outing was the annual trip down the river from Tower Pier to Southend; having taking the tram

(later bus) to the City we would join the queue for the paddle-steamer — in the early days either the *Royal Eagle* of 1932 or the much older *Golden Eagle* dating from before World War 1. My last trip was in 1963. By then the paddlers had all gone, and the ship was the *Royal Sovereign*, a handsome diesel-powered motor vessel built in 1949. Just as Green Line services were being hard hit by the motor car, so there were fewer and fewer customers for a long voyage down the Thames, particularly as foreign travel, involving taking the family car across the Channel on a ferry, was becoming common-place. Southend too was in decline as a resort, although we did the traditional Southend things like visiting the Kursaal, buying chips and taking a ride on the bumper cars. This latter was a bit of a mistake, as after one particularly satisfying wallop my girlfriend turned pale and fainted. A doctor was called who pro-

nounced her arm broken, so off we went to the Casualty department of Southend Hospital, where she was attended to. Left arm encased in plaster, she bravely insisted she could make it back to the *Royal Sovereign*, but it was with considerable apprehension that I returned one slightly damaged young lady to her mother.

• 9 •

A Brand-new Tube Line

FOR some 20-odd years Victoria had been my West End terminus. Although well served by buses we Croydonians felt, along with the citizens of Norbury, Streatham, and Brixton, that we had been left out in the cold by the Tube system. The District Line would carry us with considerable efficiency east and west from Victoria — South Kensington and its museums were only a couple of stations away — but to get anywhere else involved a fairly lengthy and roundabout Inner Circle ride. London Transport had long wanted to rectify this, and on 1 September 1968 there opened the first section of the first completely new Central London Tube line since Edwardian times.

Note 'first section', for this was the modest one linking Walthamstow with Highbury & Islington, which was very nice for North Londoners but not of any great interest to the rest of the world. What was most needed was the section from Victoria through Green Park to Oxford Circus, Euston, St Pancras and King's Cross. The section to Warren Street, one station south of Euston, opened in December 1968, and finally Victoria was reached — that is to say trains began operating — in March 1969. Now Victoria and Oxford Street were less than 10 minutes apart, and the Victoria Line did great business from Day One — although it was not, initially, very popular with elderly ladies, of whom more anon. It would be completed in the summer of 1971 with the extension to Pimlico and under the Thames to Vauxhall, Stockwell, where there was an interchange with the Northern Line (until then South London's

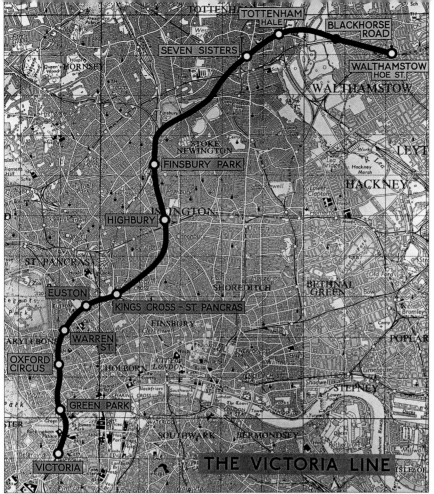

Left: The concept of the Victoria Line dated back to the 1940s. This early map shows the planned course of the line.
Ian Allan Library

Below left: Construction of the Victoria Line involved placing large canopies over the Regent Street end of Oxford Circus, requiring the temporary diversion of bus routes away from the area.
Ian Allan Library

Below: The automatic ticket machines at Seven Sisters station.
Ian Allan Library

only Tube line apart from the Bakerloo Line's three stations at Waterloo, Lambeth North and the Elephant & Castle), and Brixton.

Back to the elderly ladies. The Victoria Line trains were, in effect, driverless. Or so the 'popular' (one sometimes wonders how on earth it acquired this title) press would have the public believe. It was not just the elderly who felt somewhat apprehensive about allowing themselves to hurtle deep under London with no-one in charge. Of course, what 'driverless' actually meant was that acceleration, signal checks and station stops were all under automatic control. The trains still had a chap correctly attired in standard driver dress sitting in the cab, ready to over-ride the automatic system should it be necessary.

The trains provided for the Victoria Line are known as the 1967 stock, but would not start carrying passengers until 1968. Some 244 carriages were ordered initially from Metro-Cammell. (One wonders whether the citizens of Birmingham, seeing generations of underground trains built in their home city for service all over the world, ever considered the possibility of Britain's second city getting its own underground system; I expect they still do.) The carriages were formed into four-car units — two driving motor cars, two trailer cars — and trains normally consisted of two units. The trailer cars were provided with a great deal of standing space and 36 seats, while the motor cars seated 40 passengers. In the now standard unpainted condition the Victoria Line trains were visually a considerable advance on their immediate predecessors, featuring curved round cab windows, while the windows in the doors extended upwards into the roof, so that standard-size standing passengers could see where they were without bending their knees — always assuming they had room to do this during the rush hour. Other innovations were brilliant headlights and a much-needed public-address system.

The train operator, as the driver was officially known, was provided with a 'traction/brake controller' which regulated both speed and braking. There was also a handbrake, hydraulically powered. On the move, rheostatic braking enabled the traction motors to be used as generators. The train operator was able to communicate both with the rear cab and, most importantly, with the control room at Coburg Street, Euston. Heating was provided in the cars, controlled by thermostats. The depot was up in the far north east of the system at Northumberland (no, wait . . . not that far) Park. A connection to the rest of the London Transport system was provided with the Piccadilly Line at Finsbury Park.

The Brixton extension required another 72 cars, identical to their predecessors. The opening of the Victoria Line attracted a great deal of publicity, on account both of its at last filling a yawning geographical gap in the network and also of the technical innovations which came with it, not least the automatic nature of controlling the running of the trains. It moved the London Tube train right to the forefront of the world rapid-transit scene.

Above: HM The Queen performs the opening ceremony at Green Park on 7 March 1969. *Ian Allan Library*

Below: A train of the Victoria Line's 1967 stock when new, before exposure to the elements could weather its unpainted finish. *Ian Allan Library*

• 10 •

The Last Leylands

WITHDRAWAL of the RTLs had begun as far back as January 1958, before the newest members of the class, in store for four years, had started work. Crazily, some other 1954 deliveries were amongst the first to go, after a mere four years' service. Never as popular with drivers and the engineering departments as were the RTs, they soon found less fussy customers elsewhere. A new departure for the class with London Transport was the repainting of 18 of them in green. Put to work from Hatfield garage in July 1960, they were not popular with staff there and within a year were sent packing, being placed in the training fleet before eventual disposal. Yet another variation on the RTL

theme was the fitting (during overhaul at Aldenham in 1964) of 23 with RT10 roofbox bodies. This was done so that, when the time came for these buses to be sold, they would take with them these older bodies, the roofbox variation being on its way out. The last roofbox RTL was taken out of service, from Cricklewood garage, in October 1968, only a few weeks before the class ceased passenger work altogether. RTL543 was officially the last, finishing on the night of 29 November that year, from Willesden garage on route 176.

We take it for granted that all modern buses have both heaters and an adequate ventilation system, but although RTs were certainly well ventilated it was not

Far left: RTL 411 crosses Tower Bridge, heading for Camberwell Green on route 42. *Author*

Left: RTL1579, of the final, 1954 batch, takes a rest at Aldgate bus station in 1961. Two other RTLs are partly visible, whilst just poking their noses into the picture are an early RM and a Green Line RT. *Author*

Below: RTL68, one of the very early members of the class fitted with a roofbox body at its last overhaul, stands at a bleak-looking Becontree Heath shortly before withdrawal. It was subsequently preserved. *Ian Allan Library*

until September 1961 that heaters began to be fitted in both upper and lower saloons — and then only on Country Area buses. RFs and GSs also gained this luxury. With just one exception, no roofbox RTs nor any RTLs and RTWs were fitted with heaters, but Green Line RTs — both the originals and a further 28 repainted for Green Line duplicate and relief work in 1960 — already had them. In 1964 work began on fitting heaters to Central Area RTs.

The number in the roof had for generations been a distinctive although not universal feature on London buses but was not perpetuated with the Routemaster family. There seems to be no definitive reason why not. At one time London Transport claimed that it weakened the roof structure, but no owner of a preserved example has ever found this a problem. Then again, it was said that it was easier to change the number, the destination and the 'via' points if they were all grouped together, but one does not find this

Upper left: RTW285 on tram-replacement route 45 nearing its Camberwell Green terminus *c*1963. *Author's collection*

Below left: Victoria bus station in June 1964. A Tottenham RTW has just managed to get its nose into the picture; beyond are RM1692, RTL633 and roofbox RTL68. *D. J. Smithies*

Above: RTWs 426 and 468 of Hammersmith (R) garage pass in Kensington whilst working the 27 — a route not normally associated with the class — in the winter of 1965. *Author*

Right: Hackney's RTW276 reaches its Putney Common terminus in February 1966, shortly before Routemasters took over. *Author*

very convincing either. Perhaps, like the switch from upper to lower case for 'via' points, it was mere fashion. A few roofbox RTs were still around at the end of the 1960s, the last — a Saunders example — going in the spring of 1971. They had finished service in the Country Area early in 1964, although a few lingered on, repainted from green to red. Nearly all Country Area buses had Weymann bodies, and no Saunders roofbox bodies were painted green.

The 8ft-wide RTW class had remained intact through the 1950s and into the '60s, but, with Leylands out of favour and lots of 8ft-wide Routemasters looking for work, October 1963 saw the beginning of the end for these big all-Leylands. In that month RMs were sent to Putney garage for route 14; most of the RTWs moved south-east to Brixton, whilst four became trainers. Very much Central London buses, the RTWs were displaced from more of their traditional routes in 1964, while late in 1965 they were ousted from Battersea, Walworth and Willesden garages, rather oddly by the similarly out-of-favour RTLs. They hung on to famous route 11 until February 1966 (curiously I had seen my last LT also on the 11), but by the end of April the only examples still on passenger duties were at Brixton on the 95 and the 109. The end came on 14 May 1966, when RTW467 became the last to drive into Brixton garage, thereafter passing straight into preservation, although a number would survive in London a while longer as trainers.

Upper left: Brixton was the last garage to operate RTWs, the 109 being one of the two routes worked by the class. RTW374 stands on the forecourt of Thornton Heath garage alongside RT1688 early in 1966. Passenger service ended in May of that year. *Author*

Lower left: The other route which saw out the RTWs was the 95. RTW1 is seen at Tooting on 25 April 1965. *M. Harrison*

Above: The RTWs served for several years on trainer duties. RTW379 turns into Chiswick Works in 1969. *Author*

Right: A far-from-original RTL at work on the island of Sentosa, Singapore. *John Fozard*

Below: The 1960s saw many London buses shipped abroad, either for further public service, as in Ceylon (now Sri Lanka), or, increasingly, as tourist attractions all over the world. Here three RTs are being loaded at London Docks for Ceylon. *Ian Allan Library*

Left: Although looking the worse for wear, RTL1194 is seen in Rancho Cordova, Sacramento, California, having been exported in 1967. Sacramento, the state capital, is a real mecca for the transport enthusiast, with stern-wheeled paddle-steamers plying the Sacramento River (which eventually becomes San Francisco Bay), trams plying the city streets, the Chicago–Oakland 'California Zephyr' passing through, and the wonderful California State Railroad Museum, which modestly claims to be the 'greatest railway museum in the world'. Well, it is American! *Michael Dryhurst*

Above: RTL592 was another Leyland which left London long before it need have done. Snapped up by A1 Service of Ardrossan, it is seen some 400-odd miles north of its original home. *Author's collection*

Left: Not all of London's Leylands disappeared in the 1960s. Breakdown vehicle 1279LD, based on a PD3A/1 bus chassis, was new in 1964 and would serve until the early 1980s. *Author*

• 11 •

The Smaller Brethren Depart

THE 1960s saw the disappearance from London Transport service of a number of single-deck classes. Inevitably it tends to be the double-deckers with which most passengers, visitors to London and enthusiasts identify, and these, certainly in the 1960s, formed much the largest part of the fleet — this was especially true of red buses. Nevertheless, London Transport's single-deckers outnumbered the total fleet of most other British bus operators, so they were not exactly thin on the ground.

Most notable casualty was the T class. This went way, way back, to 1929, although, of course, the few remaining members still in service in 1960 were much more modern, being the last survivors of the final variety, the 15T13s of 1948. Always in green livery, a number had been transferred to the Kingston area, where they worked alongside RFs until September 1959. This left nine still on London

Transport books in January 1960. T787 was the last in passenger service, at Crawley, where it ceased work in August 1962.

Fortunately a number of examples remain of this extraordinarily varied class. One of the original batch delivered in December 1929, T31, was privately bought in 1956 and resides, beautifully restored to ornate General red and cream livery with cut-away open rear entrance, at Cobham and is often seen out and about. Another early one is T219, an elegant Duple-bodied Green Line coach of 1931, which is part of the London Transport Museum collection and also takes to the road from time to time. Successors of these early coaches were the somewhat bulbous-looking 9T9s, of which T448, dating from 1936, is presently undergoing restoration at Cobham. The next variation was the famous Green Line 10T10, 255 of which went into service immediately

before the War. Cobham's T504 makes frequent sorties, including regular TV and film appearances, while another 10T10 has been brought back from Australia. A most remarkable find, on a farm in France in 2003, was T357, one of the early 5T4s rebodied by Chiswick in 1935; this has since been brought back safely to Cobham and currently awaits restoration. Finally there is the postwar T792, officially described as having a provincial-type Mann Egerton body, although, being built to LT design, has always looked pure Chiswick, inside and out.

The TD, the Leyland Tiger equivalent of the half-cab AEC Regal T, did not arrive until the postwar years. A few of the final Mann Egerton 1/1TD2s lasted into the 1960s, their last duties being on the 240A from Edgware garage, where RFs replaced them in October 1962. Two — TD95 and TD130 — have been preserved.

One of the revolutionary side-engined Qs, Q75, was still London Transport property in 1960, having been converted to a mobile gas unit but managing to remain looking very bus-like. Two of these BRCW-bodied buses have been preserved.— Q55 and Q83.

Finally we must note the three members of the RW class. AEC Reliances with dual-door Willowbrook bodywork, they entered service in the Country Area in September 1960 and, although in no way veterans, were sold to Chesterfield Corporation in 1963.

Far left: One of the last survivors of the long-lived and highly varied T class was T784, a Chiswick-designed, Mann Egerton-bodied Country Area bus of 1948, seen towards the end of its life at Crawley garage. *Author*

Top: The last route to feature the TD class was the 240A from Edgware garage. These Leyland Tiger PS1s had bodywork virtually identical to that on the final batch of Ts. TD114 and TD99, seen on the forecourt of Edgware Underground station, would be taken out of service in October 1962. *Author*

Above: RW1, one of three Willowbrook-bodied AEC Reliances bought in 1960 for evaluation and tried out at various Country Area garages. It is seen here at Hemel Hempstead in August 1963. Later in the year all three, which received a pretty frosty reception from London Transport staff, took themselves up north to Chesterfield Corporation, where they proved vastly more popular, serving for another 14 years. *J. Cowdery*

• 12 •

A One-Man Revolution

WE have touched on the notion that in some respects the Routemaster was seen as old-fashioned long before it had ceased production and that elsewhere the rear-engined double-decker was becoming the norm. London has always thought of itself as unique, with operating conditions more arduous than those of any other UK city and not necessarily bound to take into account what Birmingham, Manchester, Glasgow *et al* are getting up to. Nevertheless, it decided it had better look at this new-fangled notion — which was not really all that new, for London Transport had itself

Below: New to East Grinstead, the experimental Daimler Fleetlines later ran in the Central Area. Green XF4 nears the end of its journey into London's dwindling docklands. *Author*

introduced side-, rear- and underfloor-engined single-deck and a handful of side-engined double-deck buses way back before World War 2.

In 1965 50 rear-engined Leyland Atlanteans (XAs) and eight Daimler Fleetlines (XFs) were put into service for comparative trials with Routemasters. To claim they caused a bit of a shock is an understatement. In the first place, as far as Londoners were concerned someone had remembered only at the very last minute to fit them with engines, just managing to plonk these right at the back of the chassis as they were leaving the production line. They'd also gone and stuck doors — *doors*, would you believe — at the front, thereby thwarting Londoners' time-honoured practice of jumping off buses and under the wheels of taxis at traffic lights.

The first-generation rear-engined double-deckers were among the least attractive buses ever seen on the roads of Britain, and these Park Royal-bodied efforts were no exception. They didn't have to be like that, for as early as 1962 Liverpool Corporation had shown what could be done when one of its Atlanteans, with handsome, in-house-designed MCW bodywork was exhibited at that year's Commercial Motor Show. London was a long-standing customer of MCW and could surely have asked for a modified version of the Liverpool design.

The XA/XF interior was the biggest shock of all, for it looked cheap and shoddy, way below the standards London had been used to for generations. Yet the same bodybuilder produced the Routemaster — and at the same time. Perhaps the new buses might have got away with it had they out-performed the Routemaster. But they didn't. In trials involving routes 76 and 24 the Atlantean — a ton heavier than the Routemaster — returned a fuel consumption of 6.6mpg, whilst the RML managed 7.8mpg. On top of all this the XAs proved unreliable, frequently breaking down. The Fleetlines were sent initially to East Grinstead to work the 424; it was intended that

with the upper deck closed off they would perform as OMO buses, while at peak times a conductor would be provided and both decks used. They were subsequently loaned to the Central Area, retaining green livery, and, whilst no better to look at, inside or out, than the XAs, performed rather better.

Not surprisingly, London Transport was not enamoured of the Atlantean, and no more were ordered. One notable 'first' the XAs did achieve was inaugurating one-man double-deck operation in the Central Area, XA22 moving to Croydon garage to begin work on the 233 in November 1969. Most of the class followed XA22 to its new home, whence they operated express services between central Croydon and New Addington, but all would be sold in 1973, being exported to Hong Kong. In the meantime London Transport decided to order Fleetlines, the first arriving in 1970. The original Fleetlines lasted much longer than the Atlanteans, the class not disappearing from London Country until 1981.

Top: XMS2, second of the original group of six experimental Strachans-bodied Merlins, at the Waterloo terminus of Red Arrow route 507 on 26 June 1969. There was room for 25 seated passengers and 48 standees. *H. J. Piltz*

Above: The entrance arrangement of the XMS, showing the turnstile and the ticket machine. The latter's unreliability would contribute to the Merlins' downfall. *Ian Allan Library*

The next revolution came in April 1966, when six AEC Swift single-deckers, with Strachans bodywork with seating for 25 passengers and standing room for no fewer than 48, inaugurated route 500, the first Red Arrow service. This ran from Victoria to Marble Arch, during the rush hour stopping only at Hyde Park Corner. You bought your ticket, which cost 4d, from an automatic machine as you entered — excellent when the machine worked, but too often it didn't. However, the Red Arrow concept caught on, was developed, and still, in a reduced form, works today. The buses themselves were known by London Transport as 'Merlins', this being reflected in the XMS ('experimental Merlin standee') class code. Nine more, the XMBs, were ordered for the Country Area, but only one took up work there, the remainder being repainted red, renumbered as XMSs and used on Red Arrow duties.

On 7 September 1968 seven more Red Arrow routes began and 22 OMO routes were introduced in the Wood Green and Walthamstow areas, all of which were provided with Merlins. A development of the original 15, these turned out to be the least successful mass-production buses ever to run in London. There were three varieties, the Red Arrow MBA, the virtually identical suburban MBS, with high standing capacity, and the 50-seat MB (45 in the green version, which retained the centre exit as provided on the MBAs and the MBSs). All had neat-looking MCW bodywork.

Above: The Country Area version of the prototype Merlin, XMB15 working from Garston (GR) garage, 9 April 1969. A 46-seater, it was supposed to enter service (as XMB1) in 1966 but because of disputes over one-man working did not take up work until 1967. *Author*

Below: MBA18, the first production Red Arrow Merlin to enter service, at Victoria on its first day — 29 February 1968. Union objections to the spread of OMO meant that no more Red Arrow Merlins would be licensed until August. *J. M. Banks*

The Merlin was to be the answer to diminishing passenger numbers and was intended to replace practically all the remaining RTLs and RTs. The seating capacity of the Central Area MB was only six lower than that of the RT/RTL, and this one-man bus was clearly going to be cheaper to run. Passenger numbers were declining, the unions were restless, recruiting was difficult, and, perhaps not surprisingly, London Transport management took a pessimistic view of the future. If there had been a Lord Ashfield or a Frank Pick it might have been different, and imaginative and aggressive measures might have reversed the trend. (That things could be turned around would be proven by Ken Livingstone and his team, albeit in rather different circumstances, at the end of the 1990s.) But the disastrous Merlin experiment seemed to epitomise the sad '60s and '70s.

The Merlin was too long for many London streets, and the automatic ticket machines often broke down (although probably not as often as the buses themselves). In November 1969 the first of the shorter SM class ('short Merlin') was delivered, taking up work in January 1970. However, if management thought that a mere shortening of the unwieldy Merlin would solve all its problems they would be very quickly disillusioned, not least because the more compact, 8.2-litre engine of the SM family proved, if anything, even less reliable than the 11.3-litre unit of the MB. By the early 1970s they were falling by the wayside, the ever-reliable RT had to be kept going a while longer, and the double-decker made a comeback.

Above: Not all Central Area Merlins were used on Red Arrow work, most being used on suburban routes; standee MBS200 is seen at Walthamstow when new. A neat-looking bus, much better proportioned than the prototypes, with a higher driving position (following complaints) and a Metro-Cammell body featuring a windscreen design which would become familiar in London (being used on a number of other designs, both single- and double-deck), the type nevertheless proved little short of a disaster, being considered too long for London streets and generally unreliable. *Gerald Mead*

Upper right: Three generations of London double-decker at home inside Croydon garage in 1968: XA12, RML2758 (the third-from-last member of its class, and actually newer than the XA) and RT2036. *Author*

Lower right: The shorter Swift (London Transport having now adopted the AEC model name) succeeded the Merlin, deliveries commencing late in 1969, although the type would not enter service until early 1970. The Swifts looked very much like the Merlins, but the first batch, of which SM10 was an example, was bodied by Marshall. Intended as a suburban bus, with 42 seats and standing room for 10, it is seen prior to entering service from Catford, the first garage to receive the type. The Swifts were no more successful than the Merlins — perhaps the saddest episode in London Transport's history from a design point of view — but the rest of the story belongs to the 1970s. Equally sad was that this represented the end of the long and generally illustrious association with AEC. *Ian Allan Library*

· 13 ·

Keeping a Record

Iremember trying to explain to John Wadham and Clive Gillam of Class 5, Winterbourne Primary School, sometime early in 1948 exactly what I was talking about in describing the brand-new buses, which 'looked a bit like a trolleybus' and were appearing on the streets of Thornton Heath. 'Look,' said John, 'it'll be in here,' producing from his satchel the Ian Allan *ABC of London's Transport, No 1: Buses and Coaches* (second edition). There, on page 11, was a picture of RT182, whilst on the cover was a 10T10 and another early postwar RT. The latter was almost spot-on, all except for the drooping cab window.

Below: Gaining access the London Transport Collection in Reigate garage was, for most enthusiasts, about as easy as penetrating the Kremlin. In the centre of the picture are Q55 and T219, flanked by TF77 and 'E1' tram No 1798. Author's collection

Perhaps the artist, who signed himself 'ANW' (A. N. Wolstenholme — wonder what happened to him), had had to prepare his engraving before the first postwar RTs actually appeared and based his picture on a 'prewar' one. There was also an 'ABC' of trams and trolleybuses, and with these, instead of making a lot of not always inspired guesses, we suddenly had the facts and the pictures to go with them.

By the 1960s there were probably more London bus enthusiasts than ever before, a number of them employed by London Transport, and it was felt that the time had come to form a society which would provide the most up-to-date information on the London bus scene, organise meetings and outings and even get involved in preservation. And so came into being LOTS, the London Omnibus Traction Society. Michael Widdan, writing in the 40th-anniversary edition of the Society's magazine, in the

Right: With the opening of the British Transport Museum in the former Clapham bus garage these treasures were at last on view to all. Pictured in 1969, a group from the Trinity School of John Whitgift stand beside London General B340 of 1911. *Author*

summer of 2004, tells of attending the first meeting, in May 1964, at a church hall in Greenford, which venue was soon replaced by a more convenient one in the City of London; he recalls that '. . . the turning point for membership growth was placing an advert in 1965 in the Ian Allan ABC of London Buses. LOTS was soon arranging film shows . . . by the end of the year the first sales stalls at meetings had started, [and] one of the members, the President, even owned a bus!'

Colin Derry, writing in the same issue, recalled, 'The first years of LOTS for me were exciting, not only for the formation and development of the Society, but also to record and report upon the London scene, which was vibrant with new generations of buses appearing regularly. Like all groups, we had our problems, behind and in front of the scenes, which we resolved with varying success.'

Joel Kosminsky was another who responded to the ABC advert. 'We were all younger, slimmer and had more hair. I took part in the trips, pocket money, weekend jobs and homework permitting … at one never to be forgotten meeting the then Chairman, Alan Sales, approached me and asked: "We have a vacancy for a Secretary. You seem enthusiastic — would you be interested?"

"What's involved?" I asked cautiously.

"Oh, not much."

Close to 30 years later, I am no longer Secretary, but still doing "not much".'

A number of early outings were made in the preserved 'Tunnel' STL1871. Michael Widdan recalls it 'running gently into the back of a car on the Brighton trip because its brakes were not up to scratch, and it also often needed a push-start'. Tragically this unique bus was scrapped before the 1960s were out. Another which might well have gone the same way was STL2377, which LOTS hoped to buy but declined 'when it was realised that the necessary repairs . . . were beyond the capacity of the Society and its members'. Happily STL2377 lives on, restored to a wonderful degree of authenticity at Cobham Bus Museum. This latter was founded in the 1970s, many of its members, then as now, also belonging to LOTS.

LOTS has done — and continues to do — sterling work in recording the extraordinarily diverse, complex and fascinating story of the London bus in its many forms, producing not only a monthly newsletter but a quarterly magazine and many other publications, which constitute a unique and precious archive.

Pride of place in the preservation movement must go to London Transport itself. Even before 1933 'the General' had begun a small collection of historic buses at Chiswick, and London Transport added to this. It was kept, far away from public gaze (even from the most intrepid bus-spotters), at Reigate garage. Nationalisation in 1948 meant that London Transport became part of the British Transport Commission, which set up a committee to look at the whole preservation scene. It issued a report in 1951 which eventually led to the appointment of a curator and, finally, to the unconfined joy of all enthusiasts,

to the Museum of British Transport in the redundant but modern Clapham bus garage, converted in 1951 from Clapham tram depot. The 'small relics' section was opened to the public in 1961, the entire museum in 1963, which meant one could wander around, first admiring *Mallard*, the world's fastest steam engine, and all sorts of other railway artefacts before moving on to the next aisle to renew acquaintance with the only surviving double-deck LT bus, 'E1' and 'Feltham' trams and many other treasures. Clapham proved not to be the permanent home of any of the exhibits, York eventually becoming home to the National Railway Museum, whilst the London

Transport Collection went, temporarily in the 1970s, to Syon Park and then, finally — perhaps — into the centre of London, re-opening in the former flower market at Covent Garden in 1980.

The 1960s was also a time when preservation of London buses by other than London Transport itself got underway. We have seen that it was still possible in the 1960s for a bus to reach the seemingly safe ranks of the preserved only for circumstances to bring about its downfall and extinction, such being the fate of STL1871. Another bus of similar vintage which was initially restored but eventually destroyed was STD90, one of the all-Leyland TD4s, much beloved

Above: In the 1960s the yard of Crystal Palace station became home to a number of preserved London buses. From left to right are RT44, RT1499, RTW75 and RTL343. Just visible behind RT44 on the far left is G351, the only London wartime austerity bus to survive into preservation in original condition and nowadays yet another Cobham resident. Of this group only RTL343 has not survived. *Author*

Left: Cravens-bodied RT1431, taken into preservation by LOTS in 1966, poses alongside RM1431, a newer AEC product with a stock number to match. The connection with the 36 group of routes would come full circle on 28 January 2005, when RT1431, by then owned by Ensignbus, would make a guest appearance on the last day of Routemasters on the 36. *Ian Allan Library*

Above: From time to time vehicles from the London Transport Collection are released so that the big boys and, occasionally, girls can take them out to play. Here the oldest surviving Green Line coach, T219, is carefully backed under its ornamental arch, which forms such a perfect frame, on the seafront at Brighton. *Author*

Right: Possibly the greatest authority on AEC buses and a renowned writer on public road transport, especially all aspects of the London scene since the 1950s, is Alan Townsin, seen here (right) in the 1990s with two preserved RTs in the background. *Author*

of enthusiasts as well as being very popular with drivers and engineers. On a much happier note the July 1968 issue of *Buses* reported: 'Incredible as it may seem, a 9T9 and a 10T10 have been secured for preservation. Both vehicles have been rescued from the scrapyard by enthusiasts and are to be restored. One really thought that all examples of these two types of AEC Regal had been broken up long ago.' Both found a home at Cobham and were indeed restored, the 9T9 (T448) appearing within a couple of years on the HCVC London–Brighton run and the 10T10 (T504) becoming something of a film and TV celebrity. An earlier member of the class, T219, made its first public appearance after restoration at the Brighton Coach Rally on 23 April 1961, *Buses*' then Editor Alan Townsin commenting on its 'most attractive livery' compared with an 'incredibly dull' RF standing alongside and paying tribute to John Scholes, Curator of the British Transport Museum, T219 being in his care.

The cost of buying an elderly, time-expired vehicle may not in itself be excessive, although even this can be daunting to cash-strapped teenagers (which was what some of the would-be preservationists were in the 1960s), but it is only when the bus has been safely delivered that the problems really start. There is little point in leaving the vehicle outside, so covered accommodation has to be found — not a simple matter, especially for a double-decker — and even then the bodywork needs much tender loving care to bring it back to a sound state and keep it like that, whilst mechanically the bus has to be sound if it is to be allowed out on the road.

We owe much to those in the 1960s who ensured that the vehicles saved from the scrapyard include not merely prewar examples of the London motor bus and trolleybus but also postwar members of the RT family, thousands of which had left the London Transport fleet by the end of the 1960s. The Historic Commercial Vehicle Club (now Society) was formed in 1958, and by the late 1960s its annual run at the beginning of May from London to Brighton afforded one of the best opportunities to see preserved London buses out on the road. Two sights to gladden the heart of any London Transport enthusiast — especially those who yearned for the ornate liveries of the prewar era — were the aforementioned T219, one of the original Green Line coaches which had ended its days as a bus but had been restored by London Transport to its handsome mid-1930s two shades of green and black, and STL2093, one of the all-time-classic roofbox variety, restored to red and white with silver roof and gleaming black mudguards; purists might point out that this wasn't strictly correct, as it was now in its slightly altered postwar configuration, but who cared? It evoked perfectly the heyday of the STL.

The extraordinarily protracted withdrawal of the RT family, from the 1950s to 1979, meant that it was quite possible to see both preserved examples and those still in service with London Transport heading down the A23 at this time. One Monday morning sometime in the spring of 1969, passing the time of day with Montgomery, one of my 13-year-olds at Portland Secondary Modern School, South Norwood, I asked him what he'd done at the weekend.

'Went to the seaside, Sir.'

'That's nice. How did you get there?'

'On a number 12, Sir,' which threw me slightly, for as far as I knew the route's southerly terminus was still the Red Deer, South Croydon. Then I remembered that Montgomery's dad was a conductor at Elmers End garage and that, as regularly happened, an RT which normally worked the 12 had been hired for the day. There would have been little chance of Montgomery's following in family footsteps, as the southernmost section of the 12 was shortly to go over to one-man operation (as route 12A), but the hiring of London buses for weekend trips to the seaside is a nice tradition which continues to this day.

Left: A regular in the early days of the preservation movement was STL2093. One of the classic roofbox variety, it is perhaps not quite in original condition (note the winking trafficators), but that is to split hairs; restored in 1958 to prewar livery of red and white with black lining and silver roof, STL2093 made a wonderful sight, and all credit goes to its owners whose efforts and foresight gave so much pleasure to so many. It is seen here on a London–Brighton HCVC run, speeding down the A23 south of Redhill — a road which Country Area STLs plied for many years, until the final withdrawal of the class in 1954. STL2093 is now enjoying a well-earned rest at Cobham Bus Museum, where it will one day be restored to match the superb condition of its fellow, STL2377. *Author*

Above: Less fortunate was STL1871, one of the batch with reinforced tyres and roof shaped to fit the confines of the Blackwall Tunnel, as can be seen in this picture of it in fine form, restored to prewar livery, at the end of a Brighton run. Mechanically it needed a fair amount of work, which could easily have been accomplished in this day and age, when it sometimes seems that all one needs are the remains of a chassis, a few flecks of paint and recollections of childhood travel by an old pensioner to bring back to life a long-dead London bus. But in the 1960s it was different, and, tragically, STL1871 was broken up.
Author's collection

Left: Another entrant on the HCVC Brighton run in the 1960s was the only surviving 9T9, T448, a Green Line coach with a somewhat over-designed, cumbersome front end; a few modifications resulted in its classic successor, the 10T10. This is not to say that T448 was not a worthy preservation project, and nowadays it is another Cobham resident. Behind in this view is RTL358, withdrawn in 1958 after a mere nine years' service and replaced by an identical bus which had been in store for four years — a consequence of London Transport's over-estimating its needs. RTL358 is currently owned by the 1983 Bus Club of London.
Author

Above: Three generations in Trafalgar Square in 1966: experimental Park Royal-bodied Atlantean XA10 working from Chalk Farm (CF) garage, with a Dalston RTW alongside and an RM on the 15 disappearing out of the picture. *Author*

Bibliography

London Bus Magazine (various editions), LOTS

abc London Transport Buses (various editions), Ian Allan Publishing

Cobham Bus Museum Magazine (various editions), ed Bill Cottrell

London Bus File 1955-62 by Ken Glazier, Capital Transport (1999)

London Transport Bus Garages by John Aldridge, Ian Allan Publishing (2001)

An Illustrated History of London Buses by Kevin Lane, Ian Allan Publishing (1997)

Reshaping London's Buses by Barry Arnold and Mike Harris, Capital Transport (1982)

London Transport Service Vehicles by Julian Bowden-Green, LOTS (1978)

London Transport Service Vehicles by Kim Rennie and Bill Aldridge, Capital Transport (2003)

Electric to Diesel 1935-1962 by David Stewart, LOTS (1977)

RT by Ken Blacker, Capital Transport (1984)

RF by Ken Glazier, Capital Transport (1991)

London Buses in the 1960s by Ken Glazier, Capital Transport (1998)

The London Trolleybus, Volume 1, by Ken Blacker, Capital Transport (2002)

The London Trolleybus, Volume 2, by Ken Blacker, Capital Transport (2004)

The Routemaster Bus by Colin Curtis, Midas Books (1981)

Routemaster, Volume 1 by Ken Blacker, Capital Transport (1991)

Various local and national newspapers

Unpublished private diaries

Various local timetables, maps and guides